THE 'TORO

The 'Toronto' Blessing

DAVE ROBERTS

KINGSWAY PUBLICATIONS

EASTBOURNE

First published 1994
Reprinted 1994 (twice)

ISBN 0 85476 538 7

Produced by Bookprint Creative Services
P.O. Box 827, BN21 3YJ, England, for
KINGSWAY PUBLICATIONS LTD
Lottbridge Drive, Eastbourne, E. Sussex BN23 6NT.
Printed in Great Britain.

For Sharon, Ben and Joel
whom I love and who give me support.

For George and Anna Roberts
for all they have invested in my life.

For Ian Coffey, Francis Schaeffer, John Wimber and Marc
Dupont, all of whom, in various ways, have been used to
shape my spiritual journey.

Soli Deo Gloria

Contents

	Preface	9
1.	Rumours of Revival	11
2.	Whispers of Glory	15
3.	Showers of Blessing	27
4.	A Broken-Hearted People	47
5.	The Toronto Connection	61
6.	Rodney Howard-Browne	83
7.	The Finger of God	101
8.	Shaken and Stirred	115
9.	Questions People Ask	143
10.	Wise Pastors	151
11.	Wading in the Water	169
	Bibliography	189

Preface

In the latter part of May 1994 and throughout the summer and early autumn, many churches across the United Kingdom, and around the world, were swept by a 'time of refreshing'.

People wept, people laughed and fell to the floor. Some were healed, some were convicted of their rebellious attitudes and some made peace with God and with others they had wronged.

This 'touch of God' had been encouraged and prayed for by an obscure Canadian church, the Toronto Airport Vineyard, a South African evangelist, Rodney Howard-Browne, and an Argentinian Assemblies of God pastor, Claudio Freidzon.

By early October it had touched an estimated 2,000 churches at least, and had ignited widespread debate both in the Christian and secular press. The mainstream media, including *The Observer*, *The Independent*, *Daily Mail*, *The Times* and *The Daily Telegraph* had all devoted large features to what had become known as the 'Toronto blessing'.

Although the phenomena of revival were by no means unknown to the mainly Pentecostal/charismatic churches that were involved, their intensity was unusual. Not since the 1904-08 period had the mainland British church sensed that the rain of God's Spirit was about to fall and envelop the church and then perhaps the nation.

Having been raised in a family whose background in the Faith Mission provoked interest in the Hebridean revival of 1949, I was not a stranger to talk of revival. Perhaps like many though I had become cold-hearted about the prospect of it actually happening. I felt I had to examine carefully what was going on, lest I find myself caught up in a moment of spiritual excitement that had little substance. My own teenage years in the independent evangelical wing of the church had planted a Berean attitude in my mind (see Acts 17:11). Was what was happening within a biblical ethos, glorifying Jesus and extending the kingdom?

As you read on I hope you will find a report that is 'warm, but thoughtful'. This book is by no means a definitive document. Other writers are even now working on books that will look in depth at the theological, historical and pastoral aspects of this 'time of refreshing'. This is an A-Z map. Others will compile the Ordnance Survey, with its fine detail and extended analysis.

This book aims to enquire, inform and perhaps inspire. As controversy inevitably surrounds such events, it has as one of its primary aims a desire to get beyond the immediate surface impressions we sometimes gain and help generate light rather than heat by what it reveals.

It is a document of beginnings. May God bless us with more events and stories and testimonies in the coming months than could ever be fitted into a book of this nature.

Dave Roberts
October 1994

1

Rumours of Revival

'The Holy Spirit hits South Kensington' was the front page headline in the London section of *The Independent* (21st June 1994).

It was not the first and was unlikely to be the last. London's flourishing Holy Trinity Brompton, a charismatic evangelical Anglican church, had been rocked by waves of 'holy laughter', weeping and a multitude of other phenomena during its two meetings on Sunday 29th May.

The speaker at these meetings was Elli Mumford, a member of the pastoral team at the South West London Vineyard, a growing church which meets in Putney. She had recently returned from visiting the Airport Vineyard Church in Toronto. The Airport Church had met every night, except Mondays, since January 20th. Over 30,000 had visited the church, including in excess of 2,000 church leaders.

Elli had been transformed by her visit. She had gone there feeling spiritually 'burnt out' and longing for a fresh understanding and vitality in her relationship with Jesus. As she received prayer and encouragement she discovered God anew, much of the time while 'on the carpet' prostrate before God.

'We were so preoccupied with the person of Jesus... There was a growing passion for the name of Jesus and for the beauty of his presence among his people.'

Elli later spent time reading church history, particularly Jonathan Edwards, and became convinced that the laughing, the shaking and all the other phenomena she had seen were found in the Bible and had often been witnessed in revival times.

The result for her had been 'a greater love for Jesus than I have ever known; a greater excitement about the kingdom than I ever thought possible; a greater sense that these are glorious, glorious days to be alive. I'm thrilled about the Scriptures. . . I haven't had this appetite for ministry for years. Jesus is restoring his joy, and his laughter is medicine to the soul.'

She asked the congregation to stand while she prayed that the Lord would bless them and give them all that he had.

Soon hundreds were laughing, weeping, receiving prayer and meeting with God.

Holy Trinity Brompton (HTB) was not the first church in the United Kingdom to be touched in this way, but the publication of their church newsletter detailing the events of Sunday 29th was to trigger an avalanche of publicity in *The Sunday Telegraph*, *Daily Mail*, *The Independent* and *The Times*. Christian word-of-mouth and the newspaper coverage would draw hundreds of ministers to the church in the following weeks; soon hundreds of churches were engulfed by the most intense spiritual fervour they had ever known.

In the midst of these 'days of heaven' an HTB staff member spoke of the 'Toronto blessing' and very soon the label became attached to what many believed was a special 'time of refreshing from the hand of the Lord'.

Just as Florrie Evans' heartfelt declaration of her love for Jesus in a New Quay youth meeting helped ignite the Welsh revival of 1904, Elli Mumford's unadorned and heartfelt testimony was to be like a spark to dry grass in many churches, many of whom played the cassette over the church PA system and then witnessed astonishing scenes as pastors fell off platforms and keeled over in the choir stalls.

But the momentous scenes at HTB were not the first, and the channels that God was using included an Argentinian Pentecostal pastor named Claudio Freidzon and a South African evangelist by the name of Rodney Howard-Browne.

For some who witnessed these scenes there were more questions than answers. This renewal appeared to be infectious. Where was the sovereignty of God in all of this? The phenomena of laughing, weeping, shaking, jerking and even animal noises weren't always easy for even the most liberated charismatic to accept. Some of the influential figures in this wave of change had links with the word-of-faith, health-and-wealth wing of the church, which was regarded with deep suspicion even by its charismatic/Pentecostal cousins. People had been prophesying revival for some time. How did we know that this was the real thing?

I had all these questions and more. You'll find some of my own personal pilgrimage in respect of this current 'time of refreshing' woven into the story that unfolds in the following pages.

The roots of what is happening are found in the early nineties. It's there we start as we seek to discover whether this is the renewal we've all longed and prayed for.

2

Whispers of Glory

Spring 1992

Argentinian pastor Claudio Freidzon visits the Orlando
Christian Centre and is prayed for by the flamboyant healing
evangelist Benny Hinn. It's prophesied that he will be used
in revival power in Argentina. Freidzon is also prayed for on
another occasion in a Benny Hinn meeting, by Rodney
Howard-Browne, a young South African evangelist.

Claudio Freidzon is an Assemblies of God pastor and former theology professor. His King of Kings Church grew
over four years to 2,000 people. Believing however that
something was missing in his ministry, he travelled in 1992
to Florida to see the evangelist Benny Hinn. Hinn prayed for
him and prophesied over him. Freidzon's church immediately mushroomed to 4,000 members, and he commenced a
crusade ministry that at one point filled a 65,000-seater
stadium.

People began to 'fall under the power' and uncontrollable
laughter became a trademark of the meetings.

His advice to those seeking renewal and church growth
was: 'There is no method. We must seek the presence of God.'

Like many touched by revival, he began to hold supple-
mentary meetings, because the normal meetings of his
church could not accommodate the visiting leaders from
other churches.

Redemption magazine commented: 'A hallmark of this revival is the emphasis on worship and praise. Missionaries report that the shekinah glory of the Lord seems to descend on the meetings.'

Freidzon has commented: 'The anointing comes through the praise and worship. God's presence descends as we immerse ourselves in adoring him.'

Not all who witness the strong emotions of these renewal meetings are impressed, believing that some people are simply caught up in emotion.

Redemption, responding to these criticisms of the Argentinian revival, comments: 'The emphasis on holiness, the desire of the people to praise and worship and the increase in concern for reaching others is genuine.'

On his return to Argentina Freidzon sees his Assemblies of God church grow rapidly from 2,000 to 4,000 and subsequently holds stadium meetings that attract 65,000, many of whom are caught up in 'holy laughter' or become 'drunk'. In November of 1993 he prays for a Toronto pastor named John Arnott at a pastors' conference in Argentina.

May 1992

Marc Dupont, a member of the pastoral team at the Airport Vineyard in Toronto, has a lengthy prophetic vision. In the vision he sees water falling over and onto an extremely large rock. There is a huge volume of water. He believes God is telling him that 'Toronto shall be a place where much living water will be flowing with great power, even though at the present time both the church and the city are like big rocks, cold and hard against God's love and his Spirit'. He sees this water flow out over the plains of Canada and ignite revival.

In July 1993 Dupont, while on a visit to Vancouver, is touched by a 'sense of urgency'. He foresees 'power and authority coming on the church in the Toronto area. There is going to be a move of the Spirit of God on the city that is

going to include powerful signs and wonders, such as in the
early days of the church in Jerusalem.'

April 1993

Assemblies of God pastor Karl Strader invites Rodney
Howard-Browne to hold revival meetings in the 10,000
seater Carpenter's Home Church in Lakeland, Florida. The
church has been through hard times and the congregation
has shrunk to 1,900. Within weeks the nightly meetings are
full and news of huge crowds and 'holy joy' is humming
along the charismatic grapevine. People travel from all over
the world, including the United Kingdom, to hear and witness the meetings.

July 1993

Peter Lyne, a respected charismatic leader in the United
Kingdom based at the Acorn Church, Sidcup, is on a leadership retreat. During worship and prayer, he feels the story of
Elisha in 2 Kings 3 impressed on him. The prophet warned
the king to dig ditches: 'You will see neither wind nor rain,
yet this valley will be filled with water.'

Lyne, aware of major evangelism initiatives in 1994
reflected, 'The rain is coming. Your situation may look as
dry and arid as the valley in the Negev where Elisha prophesied, but up in his mountains God is preparing the flash
floods that will change everything.'

4th October 1993

Marc Dupont, Stacey and Wes Campbell and other Toronto
area Vineyard leaders gather for prayer and fellowship.

One voice prays that there will be: 'A fresh vision that
would flood, not only from this place, from the interior of
this province, but that it would go from nation to nation to

nation to nation. And that God, your name would be lifted up. It will not be the signs and wonders, but it will be the fruit, and the fruit will remain. And it will bring righteousness and it will bring purity. It will bring holiness.'

For Carol Arnott of the Airport Vineyard there is the encouragement: 'I am bringing you to that oasis time again. A time of refreshing that comes from the presence of the Lord.'

Those gathered are reminded that Marc Dupont had prophesied that God would use John Arnott 'to administrate great outpourings of God's presence to masses of people in cities of the world'.

Hearts of faith believe it will happen, but it must seem impossible. What can catapult a 350-strong church in Canada into the forefront of a worldwide move of the Spirit of God? It takes great faith to believe, for in the natural way of things it seems unlikely.

November 1993

English visitors to Rodney Howard-Browne meetings begin to see similar phenomena in their churches. In Penzance they are laughing, but some are struck dumb for days on end. Others 'fall under the power' in a supermarket. Consistent reports are trickling into the UK of churches in the USA where laughter has dominated the meetings for weeks.

October/November 1993

John Arnott visits an Argentinian pastors' conference organised by Luis Palau's brother-in-law Ed Silvoso. He is prayed for by Argentinian AOG pastor Claudio Freidzon. It proves to be a breakthrough time for the revival-hungry Canadian pastor.

On his way back to Canada he visits an Association of Vineyard Churches leadership gathering and hears of the new power for ministry received by St Louis pastor Randy

Clark after prayer in a Rodney Howard-Browne meeting.

Clark has not found it easy to get to the place where he is ready to be blessed. The year 1993 has been a hard one and he is close to burnout. He is desperate for God's touch. He is reluctant however to go to a meeting taking place at the Rhema Bible Church, a word-of-faith style church. He feels the Lord reproves him for his 'smug' attitude and he weeps. A new man emerges – one who is ready to be the 'firelighter' at the Toronto Airport Vineyard church.

The pace of renewal is beginning to quicken. John Wimber, the international leader of the Vineyard Churches, is spending a great deal of time in solitude as he battles through cancer chemotherapy treatment. Over a period of months he feels that God has told him on twenty-seven different occasions to 'go to the nations'. He tells his fellow leaders in a leadership newsletter: 'Seventeen times he spoke in the same context and said that this would be a season of new beginnings.' The Lord is saying, 'I'm going to start it all over again. I'm going to pour out my Spirit in your midst. . . .'

Wimber does not feel up to the task physically. Like the aged Abraham and Sarah, he isn't sure whether he can help bring to birth new life. In mid-January, sitting in his Anaheim church building, he hears himself saying: 'Shall I have this pleasure in my old age?'

He remarks: '. . .the very words that Sarah laughingly said to herself when she overheard the Lord say she was going to have a son from her 90-year-old womb by her 100-year-old husband' (Gen 18:10). He feels this is a word of life from the Lord and is deeply touched.

December 1993

Argentinian associates of Claudio Freidzon visit a south-coast town. One minister and his wife, neither of whom have 'fallen under the power' in thirty years of charismatic/Pentecostal involvement, spend most of the evening on the carpet.

They hardly feel able to drive home.

5th December 1993

John Wimber feels that the Holy Spirit tells him to 'stir up the gifts of the Spirit that our people may have a greater hunger for the giver, Jesus'. The Anaheim Vineyard sets aside Sunday night for that purpose.

December – Toronto

John Arnott has someone, a stranger, visit him at the church office. The stranger tells him that he's been running with the footmen, but he's going to ride with the horsemen.

A visiting speaker, Larry Randolph, tells the church that a great anointing is coming and that it's almost here.

John Arnott regards these prophecies as a help in terms of 'catalysing my own faith'. Several of the recent prophecies have had the same theme. Like many, Arnott likes to weigh and consider prophecy and wait and see. He and his wife Carol have good reason to take Mark Dupont seriously. Carol has asked God to confirm a major move in their lives via Mark as a sign that he is a genuine 'hearer from God'. It happens and the Arnotts take him seriously.

16th January 1994

John Wimber believes God has given him the word 'Pentecost'. He spends hours seeking the Lord for further insight, but none comes until he has a 'vision of young people in a certain set and order' during the evening meeting.

He later asks the young people to come forward. 'They did and the Lord came, consuming them in a beautiful and powerful way. It began a significant increase of the outflowing of the power at Anaheim.' It is still flowing in May as John writes these words to the Vineyard leaders worldwide.

20th January 1994

A four-night series of meetings at the Toronto Airport begins. The speaker is Randy Clark of the St Louis Vineyard. John Arnott is awe-struck at the response as the normal 'handful' who receive prayer swells to embrace the entire congregation. He doesn't let Clark go home at the end of the weekend and eventually flies Clark's wife up to be with him as the meetings look set to enter a third week. Laughter, prostration, 'drunkenness' and other physical phenomena are the initial hallmark of the renewal, but it soon becomes apparent that people are having profound experiences while on the carpet – including visions – that are bringing internal change as well as outward excitement. One girl who has a vision of family members in heaven with God feels prompted to go to the hospital and pray for her chronically sick, near-blind, vegetative-state friend. Within three hours her sight returns and she emerges from her coma-like state. In the ensuing weeks several family members come to Christ.

This is only a beginning. The Vineyard Church grapevine in the United States begins to hum. The British Vineyard movement is small, only seven churches, but there are literally thousands of sympathetic British churches which are influenced by the Vineyard. The trickle of British visitors to Canada soon rises to twenty or thirty a week, and the seeds of a 'time of refreshing' in the British Isles are sown.

Spring 1994

Terry Virgo, leader of the New Frontiers network, which drew over 150 churches to its 1994 Bible Week, returns to his Columbia church in America after a trip to South Africa to discover that many in the congregation have experienced 'a new encounter with God in the power of the Holy Spirit' at Rodney Howard-Browne meetings in St Louis. Writing in

Frontline, Terry speaks of 'extraordinary sights in terms of people being filled with the spirit of joy and "drunkenness". We have also seen lives totally transformed – people have a new hunger for God and a new zeal to see him glorified. I have never seen lives changed so rapidly and the atmosphere of a church altered so swiftly.'

Another New Frontiers leader, Dave Holden of Sidcup Community Church, is in Columbia at the moment of renewal. He does not experience significant physical manifestations, but is greatly used on his return to England.

Terry Virgo visits England in May and meets with a small group of leaders from the New Frontiers network. 'We had two days of amazing experiences of God's presence and a release of prophesying such as I have never known.'

After that comes 'an unforgettable evening' in the 900-strong Church of Christ the King in Brighton – Terry Virgo's home congregation in the UK.

'Following this, over two hundred full-time elders from New Frontiers gathered for two days of prayer and fasting. . . Once again the Spirit of God was poured out in phenomenal measure.'

Greatly refreshed, Terry Virgo feels that God is telling him, 'I have attended a lot of your meetings, now I am inviting you to attend some of mine.'

7th May 1994

Following the Sunday evening service, a young woman in the Queen's Road Baptist congregation in Wimbledon has 'a profound sense of God's glory'. The pastor, Norman Moss, finds her in the church on her knees, telling God how sorry she is. She has a vivid picture of the congregation kneeling in repentance. The congregation returns and many fall to their knees and begin to ask God for forgiveness. The congregation later joins hands and prays around the building and then takes communion together. The meeting doesn't finish until nearly 11.00 pm.

The following Sunday the congregation meets again after the evening service. They worship together, but worship leader Malcolm Kyte falls to the floor and 'didn't or couldn't' get up again for an hour and twenty minutes. People are laughing, crying and shaking. Pastor Norman Moss had visited the Toronto Airport church in mid-May.

The Wimbledon church is not alone. The Church of Christ the King in Brighton has a warning prophetic word that God is going to 'disrupt' them. John Hosier, the pastor of the church, takes this seriously enough to call a special prayer meeting. 'Over 400 attended. We had a strong sense that this was a special time of meeting with God.'

In rapid succession the church is visited by Terry Virgo and then one of their own leaders, Alan Preston, who is fresh from a visit to the Toronto Airport church. Joy and loss of bodily strength are much in evidence.

Speaking to *Alpha* magazine as the month of May ended, John Hosier comments, 'We know that there is always flesh and spirit in these things and for some suggestible people there will be an experience but little change. We are hearing many testimonies however of a sense of an encounter with God, an increase in prayer and Bible reading, a boldness in witnessing. We've seen our Sunday evening congregation double.'

Is this revival? John Hosier is cautious: 'I would describe it more in terms of days of refreshing from the hand of the Lord.'

In Toronto, baptist pastor Guy Chevreau describes it as a renewal, not a revival: 'This is for the church and for the prodigals.'

Revival fire

Many whom the Holy Spirit has used in the United Kingdom have never been to Toronto or been prayed for by Rodney Howard-Browne. God touched several churches prior to any contact with anyone else, preparing them for what was to come.

The history of revival would seem to indicate that God will often use human agencies as channels for his blessing. During the 1949 revival in the Hebrides it did not break out simultaneously all over the Islands. Revival came to the parishes where fervent prayer was offered and usually where the Revd Duncan Campbell spoke.

In the 1859 revival in Ulster the spark was lit in Connor, then spread to Ahoghill, when some Connor people led a well-known Ahoghill sinner to Christ. As the revival engulfed Ulster people travelled from all over Britain, Europe and America to witness what God was doing.

In 1904 Alexander Boddy, Vicar of All Souls Parish Church, Sunderland, travelled to Wales to discover what God was doing there. He was later used to spark a revival in Sunderland that helped launch the British Pentecostal movement. Meanwhile in Los Angeles, Frank Bartleman, part of the coming Azusa Street revival, distributed 5,000 pamphlets on 'The Revival in Wales'. T.B. Barratt didn't visit Asuza Street but he wrote to them. They encouraged him to seek God as never before. He received a fresh empowerment and was to be used mightily in the 1907 revival in Sunderland.

When Azusa Street experienced revival in 1906, people travelled from Africa, India and all around the world. So the phenomena of people 'chasing' the presence of God is not unknown.

Toronto is only one small piece in the jigsaw of God's move in 1993/94. It is not and never has been necessary to go there, but for desperate, hungry Christian leaders it has proved to be a place of retreat. Many, free from their daily tasks, have been able to spend hours in prayer and study. Away from their home church they have allowed themselves to be spiritually vulnerable.

Some may deplore the weekly exodus to Toronto. One

doesn't have to go to Toronto. But it would seem to have been part of God's provision for many.

24th May 1994

Elli Mumford meets with several leaders of Holy Trinity Brompton and its satellite congregations. Among the leaders is Nicky Gumbel. As Mumford prays, the glory falls and Gumbel doesn't make it to the staff meeting at HTB. He rushes in at 2.00 pm and is asked to close the meeting in prayer. He does so, but as he prays the Spirit sweeps in and the meeting carries on until 5.00 pm.

Nicky consults with Sandy Millar, the highly regarded vicar of Holy Trinity Brompton, and it is decided that Elli should preach on Sunday 29th May at the church.

The rest, as they say, is history.

3

Showers of Blessing

As editor of *Alpha* magazine, one of Britain's leading evangelical monthlies, I had planned to write about the Argentinian revival and Rodney Howard-Browne since February, but hadn't felt the timing was right. Then I planned to do something in August, but our designer, Rachel Salter, urged me to go for July, despite the fact that we had only a few days before the magazine went to print.

That night my own pastor, Martyn Relf, told me about the prophecy of a Kent-based Strict Baptist pastor, David Obbard. A prophetic vision detailed in his autobiography *Ploughboy to Pastor* (published privately) suggests that revival would start in 1994. Obbard was studying Ezekiel 37 one day in 1954. He wrote:

> It came to me in this way; that as bone came to bone, so there would be a revival of interest in the doctrines of grace, which are surely the framework of the true church, but this would not bring revival itself. Also, as the sinews and flesh came upon them, so there would follow a revival of true biblical order and experiential spiritual life, but neither would these things bring revival. Following this there would be a mighty movement of the Holy Spirit, the breath of God, and the church would be raised from its lifeless state to that of an exceeding great army.
>
> When this persuasion came to me there was presented to my mind the figure of twenty-year periods: twenty years for the

bones to come together, twenty years during which Bible-based churches of born-again believers would be established on a worldwide scale; and some time during the next twenty years [ie from 1994 onwards] a mighty outpouring of the Holy Spirit. I can give no reason for these twenty-year periods other than to repeat that they were presented to my mind at that time.

Obbard, reflecting in the early 1990s, pointed to the ministry of Martyn Lloyd-Jones as evidence of the promotion of doc-trines of grace. He pointed to the growth of the charismatic movement as a factor in 'a return to the New Testament pat-tern of church life' and he expressed his hope for the period from 1994 to 2015.

Perhaps this was it.

We prepared a four-page article for the magazine, tracing the roots of what was happening, the historical precedents and using the reflections of revival writer Jonathan Edwards.

A rumour of revival was spread abroad by the editorial. The magazine came out on 17th June. The Christian media and the mainstream press were full of similar rumours of revival that weekend.

The *Church of England Newspaper* (17th June 1994) breathlessly reported 'Revival breaks out in London Churches'. In careful prose they reported: 'It is said that the charismata, or the gifts of the Holy Spirit – talking in tongues, prophetic talents and physical sensations – which were granted to the disciples on the first Pentecost, are being more keenly felt by churchgoers than ever before.'

A service at Holy Trinity Brompton was said to have ended in chaos as dozens burst into spontaneous laughter or tears, trembled and shook in their seats or fell flat on the floor.

The paper assured readers that 'the clergy are acutely aware that such unusual goings-on can be offputting and divisive and are taking steps to reassure dubious parish-ioners'. HTB Vicar Sandy Millar noted, 'The non-believers usually think it's fine. They think if there is a God, then he's likely to act in unusual ways.'

The national newspaper reporters were perhaps more bemused. Andrew Brown of *The Independent*, no friend of the Pentecostal excitement of Morris Cerullo or Reinhard Bonnke, liked the 'cogent, well modulated and practical' sermon he heard at St Paul's Onslow Square, and the 'un-hysterical fashion in which everything happened' (*The Independent* 21st June 1994).

Brown was faintly amused by the children's knowing attitude in the midst of it all. Following their Sunday school 'they ran down the side of the church, apparently taking no notice of what was going on. . . This was, after all, an Anglican church in the heart of South Kensington. . . If people were going to faint, shake and laugh like drunks, this was no excuse for staring.' He noted that the church, in spite of all this interior personal excitement, had just given £4,000 for Rwandan relief work.

Ruth Gledhill writing in *The Times* (18th June 1994) was not so sanguine. 'A religious craze that originated in Canada and involves mass fainting and hysterical laughter has crossed the Atlantic. . .' This first paragraph betrayed the tone of a feature that was not a big winner in the neutral reporting stakes.

The Sunday Telegraph was a little more enthusiastic, having commissioned a report about the Toronto Airport Vineyard, which appeared on Sunday 19th June under the headline 'Faithful fall for the power of the Spirit'. The well-informed writers, Fred Langan and Paul Goodman, reflected that some Christians feared that this 'time of refreshment' could 'degenerate into emotionalism and self-indulgence' and become just 'another aspect of the modern search for self-fulfilment'.

Clive Calver, General Director of the Evangelical Alliance, expressed the belief that internal transformation could be 'accompanied by a new commitment to social action, such as care for the poor and homeless. If this happens, it's nothing but good news.'

Another *Telegraph* writer visited Holy Trinity Brompton to 'watch the faithful giggle their way along the path of righteousness'. When the prayer started he beat a hasty retreat to the back but eventually he consented to be ministered to. 'They prayed. I repented.' He left the church dazed, his scepticism apparently dented but not quite demolished.

What would the *Daily Mail* (20th June 1994) make of it all, given their predisposition to Evangelical-baiting? Tony Holpin noted the usual phenomena, but reported that 'members of the congregation were at pains to stress that they are neither fanatics nor prone to hysteria. They spoke of being consumed by a warm feeling of love and peace.'

On the 24th June HTB staff member Mark Elsdon-Dew reassured the *Church Times*: 'Please emphasise that this is not so bizarre or outrageous that sensible people won't want anything to do with it. We try to show common sense and order, but if it is God it would be awful not to have all that he offers.'

All this media attention had two effects. It galvanised the Christian grapevine into frenetic activity, resulting in many pastors visiting Holy Trinity Brompton, and it also brought the 'glums' out of their closets. 'This can't be the real thing,' they reasoned. 'In revival people repent and weep – not laugh.' Soon opinions were appearing in letters pages and church circulars based on these newspaper reports. There was talk of 'spirits of deception' and 'spiritual lunacy'.

It was unfortunate that this should be so. The mainstream press did not have the complete story, nor did they do much beyond reporting the physical phenomena and the clergy response. The hidden story was deeper and more significant and more than an antidote for those who were fretting about superficiality. Those in the midst of renewal were well aware of the perils and the pitfalls but believed that God would bring forth good fruit.

St George's in Ashtead was touched by renewal after the congregation listened to a tape of Elli Mumford speaking at

Holy Trinity Brompton. The rector, Chris Hughes, writing on the 25th June said, 'Members of the church in Ashtead tell of knowing a new joy in their Christian faith, a renewed love for God, a sense of fresh purpose in their lives, a strengthened resolve to follow Jesus Christ, healing of long-standing problems and a greater peace.'

At the 200-strong Baptist church in Little Bookham, Surrey, revival and renewal came as the church searched their hearts over future direction and their evangelism strategy. They set aside a week for daily prayer in late May. The pastor, Ian McFarlane, felt a strong sense of the Spirit's burden for a number of days and found himself literally trembling. Finally he committed to paper a prophetic word he believed the Lord had given him.

He arranged to share this at a special after-church meeting. He had received a tape of Elli Mumford speaking at Holy Trinity Brompton which he played to the after-church meeting. Ian takes up the story: 'I asked the congregation to stand and wait on the Lord. Within seconds, I pitched off the platform. I was unable to move, but was aware of my surroundings. Eventually I was able to stand again and discovered prayer and ministry taking place all around me.'

Ian noticed immediate fruit. 'The people can't wait to get to worship. They're more open about their faith and there is a new passion for the friendship and community evangelism we're involved in.'

Coverage in the local newspaper led to witnessing opportunities for church members, including Mrs McFarlane on her regular visit to the local hairdresser.

Phil Rees of South Street Baptist in Greenwich had never seen anything like it in thirty years of church life. His church is part of the Ichthus network in south London. Ichthus leader Roger Mitchell had attended the same conference in Argentina as John Arnott, and some of the Ichthus churches had been experiencing a 'time of refreshing' since December 1993.

Phil reflected: 'The Lord takes over – you can hardly believe it. There have been tears of repentance and a release of tension. There's a growth of holiness and dwelling close to God. The last seven weeks have been the best in my Christian life.'

Gerald Coates, leader of the Pioneer network of churches, returned to his Cobham-based congregation after visiting a Swedish conference where similar things were happening. He carefully avoided mentioning the phenomena or placing hands on people when he prayed for them. He tells of one man he prayed with:

> He was a man of great control. He came to me and told me he didn't want to live with temptation any more. He's never fallen under the power of the Spirit in the fifteen years I've known him. He went down in thirty seconds. He was weeping under conviction. He told me later he was overcome with a sense of the awesomeness of God. He could not move, although he was aware of what was going on in the meeting.
>
> There's a sense of the presence of God among the people here. They don't want to live with sins they've previously tolerated. One person spoke to me of the feeling that they were experiencing a strong sense of both the fear of the Lord and the joy of the Lord in a way they had never known before.
>
> We are also seeing people coming to salvation – including twenty-five at a recent meeting led by Steve Clifford.

Dave Holden, pastor of the Sidcup Community Church, has also seen change in people's lives. 'When we pray for them they laugh or weep. In the following days they talk of a sense of God's presence, their marriages being different, ethical change in their lives. We have discovered a new lease of life. Our prayer meetings have quadrupled.'

The laughter in meetings may not have seemed funny to some, but there have been some genuinely humorous moments.

An ambulance arrived at a Sidcup meeting to pick up

someone who had been taken ill. The ambulance men entered the hall and witnessed a scene where dozens were on the floor in various stages of spiritual encounter. 'Which one's ours?' they asked, somewhat bemused.

At another Sidcup meeting there was prayer for a Jehovah's Witness, who immediately slumped to the ground. While he was 'out' those praying for him prayed vigorous Trinitarian prayers. He stirred and they talked to him about faith. He indicated that he was searching but had not found satisfaction with the JWs. They explained the gospel to him and he gave his life to Christ. They prayed again that he would be filled with the Spirit. He spoke in tongues and fell to the floor again. He eventually stirred and seemed keen to leave the meeting. He had been there two hours. Pressed as to what the hurry was, he indicated that his girlfriend was waiting for him in the car. He had evidently not anticipated staying very long.

South African evangelist Rodney Howard-Browne drew attention to a woman in the front row of the Carpenter's Home Church meetings, who had been stopped by the police. She had been overcome by laughter as she listened to Howard-Browne on the radio. A policeman noting her unsteady driving had stopped her. With some difficulty she wound the window down. The policeman, convinced she was drunk, sought to remove her from the car. The moment he touched her, he began to laugh and was unable to do anything for several minutes. When he regained his composure, Rodney (on the tape) was at the appeal stage of his sermon. The policeman, a backslidden Pentecostal, began to weep. The lady led him back to the Lord and then helped him back to his patrol car.

Another story involves a lady in similar circumstances asked to undertake a breathalyser test. As she blew into the bag, the policeman fell to the ground laughing. At Claudio Freidzon's meetings in Argentina a special taxi service helps weakened believers get home. Holy Trinity Brompton have

the number of a taxi firm which understands that its parish-
ioners are 'not drunk as you suppose' and are safe to have in
the taxi.

There are other stories circulating that would seem to
have little basis in truth, including the infamous 'angelic
messenger' story. This involves people on a journey picking
up a hitchhiker or getting into conversation with someone
who tells them Christ is returning soon and that what is happening is preparation. The 'angel' often disappears from the
back of the car while it's cruising at 70 mph. A variation on
this story has been told in a south west London church and
alluded to in the Holy Trinity Brompton magazine.

This is the stuff of urban legend. Not improbable if you
have a Christian worldview, but well documented in folk-
lore literature. In view of the fact that such stories have circulated among English Evangelicals for over fifteen years,
they do need to be taken with a pinch of salt. Can your
source name the people involved? Unless you see or hear of
a named individual, who has prepared a signed testimony
and has two people prepared to vouch for their integrity, then
you should gently encourage those who retell the story to be
aware that it might be a myth.

Stories were flooding in from around the country that
were well verified and profoundly moving.

Leaders such as Gerald Coates (Pioneer People) and Bryn
Jones (Covenant Ministries) had travelled to Birmingham to
hear Rodney Howard-Browne speak at a series of meetings
in early June. They were uniformly positive about Rodney
himself, but not all had found the meetings easy. Browne did
all the praying, and the effect on some people was unusual.
Bryn Jones received prayer at the Friday morning meeting.

Gerald and Bryn, early allies in the New Church movement of the seventies, had long been wary of each other.
Peace had recently broken out, however, and Gerald visited
a Covenant Ministries leadership gathering at this time.

Scenes of repentance and empowerment, laughter and

joy, already apparent among some in the Covenant group, exploded out across the network. The summer issue of *Covenant News* was full of joyful reports.

At the Cardiff church, senior elder Peter Grearley reported:

> People have been falling over, laughing uncontrollably, rolling around drunk and crying deeply. We have been unable to end some meetings because the people don't want to stop praising God or leave his presence.
>
> As we worshipped last Sunday, Agnes Morris was instantly healed of a twenty-year back problem. She had been unable to bend properly and is now a living testimony to God's healing power.

At the King's Church in Loughborough, Rena Tsikli, a lady of Greek origin, was praying when she heard a man speaking in tongues behind her. The man didn't know the Greek language but what he spoke, when translated, meant 'take it upon you'. She went forward to drink from a glass of water, a symbolic act of faith for those wishing to receive from God. 'As I drank, the Spirit moved me to tears. My hands tingled and I began to shake. I could no longer stand and fell to the ground.' She wept for some time.

The pastor Gareth Duffty had another amazing story to tell. 'Abigail, our eight-year-old, told four of her school friends what had happened at the Sunday morning meeting. They asked to know Jesus for themselves, so she prayed with them, laid hands on them to receive the Holy Spirit and they fell down under the power of God. They said that their knees had turned to jelly. My wife Sandra has been approached by parents wanting to know more as children have gone home with stories of their experiences.'

The King's Church was not the only church in Loughborough being touched by God. Roy Monks, the pastor of the Elim Pentecostal church, told *Direction* magazine that a friend had told him in mid-June what was happening around the country. Roy's comment was, 'I just pray that God does not pass us by.' He went to the normal 9.15 am service. At the 11.15 service things suddenly became different. There was a tremendous awe, and sense of the presence of God. After some time Roy asked people forward for prayer, and immediately people began to fall down under the power of God. Whole groups of the congregation fell without anyone being near them. There was a lot of crying, and a lot of heart-searching. God was obviously present. Roy said, 'I just felt I could not close the service at the normal time, and it went on until about 2.00 pm.' At the evening service Gordon Neale spoke on 'the River of God', and again people were invited out for prayer: similar things happened.

During the following weeks things seemed quite normal. The services were good, but nothing unusual happened. Then Roy met with three other local ministers for prayer and discussion. While they were praying one of the ministers, a Baptist, fell under God's power. Roy felt he should prophesy over him, and the minister confirmed that someone else had already given him the same prophecy. Roy then felt he should prophesy over David Hadden, and again David confirmed that what Roy had prophesied had been given to him by two other people. Roy was so overcome by the obvious accuracy and confirmation of the prophecies that he began to weep.

The Baptist minister described how, at the close of the service the following Sunday, a quiet lady came from the congregation and said that she felt God wanted them to continue in prayer for a while. He felt this was right, and encouraged the congregation to do so. Within minutes almost the whole congregation was swept off its feet, overcome with tremendous laughter.

At a united church meeting in Loughborough a day or two later, similar things began to happen – and again at their own services the following Sunday. 'The amazing thing,' said

Roy, 'is that the most unlikely people seem to be receiving the experience. It is not just the normally excitable type of people, but businessmen, university lecturers and the like, many of them very dignified and normally quiet people.'

Direction also noted that at a recent meeting in Bridgend it was reported that there was a tremendous storm. The rain began to pour down on the roof with deafening power. At the very same moment, the whole congregation felt the 'rain of God' hit the place, and experiences similar to those described above took place. At a Brethren church in Diss, Norfolk, where traditionally people had been somewhat sceptical about the Pentecostal phenomena, God moved into a meeting as on the day of Pentecost, and they all began to speak in tongues. They had to invite a Pentecostal speaker to come and teach on the subject.

Dorian Hammond, leader of Highdown Church, Worthing, saw immediate fruit from his own encounter with God. He made contact with eleven young men, all with a background in the occult. 'Already four of them have been saved, delivered and filled with the Spirit.'

And still this wave of the Spirit rolled on.

The Salvation Army is no stranger to the 'touch of God'. Some of its older churches have shelves at the back where they used to lay people who had been 'prostrated'.

As the autumn approached, its UK leader, Commissioner Pender, encouraged corps around the country to observe the Gamaliel principle (see Acts 5:34-39) – if it was not of God, it would come to nothing; if it was God at work, it would be foolish to oppose him! At a leadership conference at Swanwick people began to fall to the floor during the worship. No one was praying for them, and there was no exhortation from the platform. Many testified to healing or restoration. One delegate, on returning to work, was asked what had happened to him over the previous days, such was the change in his countenance. Phil Wall, Salvation Army National Evangelist, was clear about the fruit. 'There's a greater passion

for Christ and the lost. Some of the people touched have
been among our most conservative leaders.'

The wave began to touch Northern Ireland in July during
the Hillsborough Bible Week, as Norman Robertson spoke
to over 800 adults on 'the Anointing'. Another wave rolled
in when twelve leaders connected with the Christian Fellowship Church returned from a visit to the Toronto Airport
church. The pastor, Paul Reid, had been radically affected
and his team had not always found it easy to come to terms
with their usually controlled pastor's 'drunkenness'.

Reflecting on the impact of his visit he concluded:

I feel God was doing many things in my life and in the rest of us
– not least the breaking of control. The Lord was saying,'I want
my church back', thus dealing a blow to my pride but also
bringing a fresh sense of his love and intimacy with him as my
heavenly Father.

We arrived back on a Saturday and our first service was on
Sunday at 9.30 am, followed by another at 11.30 am. After the
singing of one song I fell over, along with several other people.
It all began to happen. People fell, laughed, cried, shook, wept,
cried out, prophesied, without anyone near them. It was a sovereign move of the Holy Spirit, and although exciting, at times
terrifying. I managed to get up to try and share but shook so
much I had to be led down from the pulpit where I lay for four
hours on the ground while all heaven broke out round about me.
We now have three meetings on a Sunday and one on a Thursday evening. If we had meetings every night of the week I sus-
pect that people would still come. We have about 2,000 adults
coming during the week, many of them visitors from other
churches.

The exciting thing is that several churches of the main
denominations have come on board in what God is doing. And
it is so thrilling to meet with Presbyterians, Church of Ireland,
Methodists and Roman Catholics, where God is moving afresh
in their churches and in their lives. I believe that a sign in the
natural – the IRA cease-fire – is a pointer to what is happening
in the spiritual. I do believe that God is moving in the land in

Ireland at this time and I don't think anyone can refute that God is on the move afresh. The meetings continue and the fire continues to fall and we believe that the intensity of what is happening will increase.

The exciting thing is that these things are happening even when people have no prior knowledge of what is going on. I went to a small country meeting in County Antrim last Saturday night, having been booked to speak about six months ago. After speaking on the love of God for a few minutes I asked people to stand – all those who wanted a fresh touch of God's love. About eighteen people came out and stood in a line and I began to pray. Without any prior knowledge of such things they fell, they shook, they cried, they wept and God came upon them in a sovereign way. I am convinced this is a move of God.

The Catholic Charismatic community in Northern Ireland was not the only Catholic group being touched during the summer of 1994.

The Cor Lumen Christi group organised a rally for Catholic charismatics in Guildford on Friday 8th July. Three hundred and fifty people attended from as far away as Westminster and Portsmouth. After explanation and testimony they 'invited the Holy Spirit to come on the whole congregation. For the next two-and-a-half hours God poured out his Spirit as many people rested in the Spirit, shook, wept and laughed, as God blessed, refreshed and healed.'

In the midst of all this fervour and excitement there were those who, while not inclined to a negative judgement, were nevertheless a little sceptical. Holy Trinity Brompton churchwarden Ken Costa was one such person. 'I had heard that there had been an outbreak of some giddiness among the members of staff at Holy Trinity Brompton. I thought, "Oh well it's a passing phase. If they want to lie about giggling, let them lie about giggling." I sort of felt a little outside it all. I thought it was a mild dose of hysteria and it would all pass over.'

Nevertheless he led a meeting at St Paul's Onslow Square

where, despite his own best efforts, he was overcome with laughter. He didn't quite know what to make of it.

He had an opportunity to visit the Toronto Airport Vineyard. He told the audience at a seminar on the Focus '94 Bible week:

> I listened to the worship – which was indifferent. I saw people shrieking and roaring and falling over and I thought, 'Well, there we are – a mild outbreak of giddiness. All of this will end.'
>
> The next morning I was sitting in the meeting minding my own business when suddenly I started shaking in every part of my body and bouncing up and down like a pogo-stick. I said 'God what are you doing?' But he didn't stop – and it carried on for two or three sessions.
>
> Now I mention this to you really just to say that I had come from a position of some scepticism. But I have now been, in the words of C. S. Lewis, 'surprised by joy'.
>
> Why does God allow this sort of shaking? I think he does it to draw attention to himself.
>
> I suspect this is a prophecy of God shaking me – my life, my control, my vested interest, my determination to run my life by what I understand.

R.T. Kendall, Minister of Westminster Chapel and highly respected Bible teacher, also felt humbled by the Holy Spirit. He was frank about it when he talked with Wallace Boulton of *Renewal* magazine.

> I have had to make a public climbdown. If you had put me on a lie detector when I first heard about it, and asked me if I thought this was of God, I would have said no. Two weeks later I changed my mind.
>
> I saw one of my closest friends, who wasn't all that open to it, fall flat on his face for ten or fifteen minutes when he was prayed for in my vestry.
>
> The man who prayed for my friend had come to pray for me, which he did. But my friend said he would allow himself to be prayed for, not expecting anything to happen. He had only

heard of Toronto that morning from me.

He was the one who fell flat on the floor, not me. That impressed me.

RT subsequently invited Sandy Millar, Vicar of Holy Trinity Brompton. He told *Renewal*:

> I had been prayed for by a number of people. Sandy Millar was the first, then Roger Forster and Ken Costa and two or three others from the staff of Holy Trinity, Brompton.
>
> Nothing happened. My wife joined us as they were praying for me. After about two minutes she was on the floor. I had never seen such a radiant smile on her face.
>
> She wept, she laughed – and she said to me later that if this was what being 'slain in the Spirit' was, she could see why people wanted it.
>
> Then, on the evening that Sandy Millar and his staff came to our church, we were about to go home when one of them asked if he could pray for me. I said, 'Sure, but I must tell you I've been prayed for many times.' I didn't want him to get his hopes up.
>
> Within a minute or so, my mind became so relaxed. The best way I can describe it is to say it was like when I had sodium pentathol years ago when I had major surgery. Yet I wasn't unconscious. I felt myself falling forward.

Did he have a great sense of God? 'No more than I had felt all day: it had been a great day for me.' What, then, was the meaning of this experience? 'For me, it was so humbling. I think God was wanting to teach me to be humbled, to look stupid and to be a fool. There I was, on the floor in front of all my deacons and their wives. There were only a couple of others to whom it happened that evening and I was embarrassed. I think that was what God wanted to do to me.'

As the summer wore on, a slowing down was expected by many. People were on holiday. For some, however, their holiday included a church camp. Seven thousand people crammed into the New Wine Bible week. On the final night Barry Kissell, part of the leadership team at St Andrew's Chorleywood saw the 'glory of the Lord' sweeping from the back to the front of the meeting. The previous week the same church had sponsored Soul Survivor, a 4,000-strong camp for young people. During the fourth song on the first night people began to fall, weep, laugh and need prayer. As the weekend progressed they took to putting the preachers on at the beginning of the meeting, before the spiritual fervour erupted.

On the Sunday night the preacher spoke valiantly over several laughing, roaring young people. (Standing at the side of the room, I for one resisted the temptation to place the right hand of fellowship over the mouth of one young 'lion'.) Children were also touched quite profoundly at the New Wine week. Captain Alan Price of the Church Army had overall responsibility for the 1, 000 or more children.

David Gardner, Minister of Burwell Baptist, Cambridgeshire, was part of the teaching team and told the *Baptist Times* about what occurred as the week progressed.

> The first evening session of the week was centred on the significance of the cross, and there was opportunity for children to pray a prayer of commitment to Jesus as their Saviour and Friend.
>
> Later in the week there was teaching about the Holy Spirit, and opportunity to respond to Christ. This was done very sensitively and, as the children waited on the Lord, some unusual phenomena began to happen. Some children began to cry (later on they said they were not sad or frightened but very happy); some began to shake and some began to laugh. I know laughing and giggling are contagious, but I believe there was much that was of God.
>
> And children did fall on the floor, resting in the Spirit; some of them heard the voice of Jesus and saw pictures or visions.
>
> Let me describe a series of pictures that one nine-year-old in my group saw as he slumped to the ground each evening.

The first time he saw lots of angels and heard a voice saying that they were there to protect him through his life. On the second occasion he saw angels everywhere, and a much larger person above them all who was in charge of them. He was told that this larger person was Jesus.

On the fourth occasion, he said he heard no voices, and saw no pictures – he was just speaking in tongues. On the fifth occasion, he saw a picture of Satan in a cage and, as Christians marched around singing praises to the Lord, Satan got smaller and smaller. When Satan was the size of an ant, he was stamped on, and disappeared.

All this from a very normal lad of nine years who was also full of fun and mischief. I do not think he could have made it up, and I do not think it came from the devil, either. All in all, a truly remarkable week.

Dave Holden, a leader in the New Frontiers network, pointed to an escalation in response and ministry on the night of the Stoneleigh Bible Week when American pastor C.J.Mahaney preached on the cross. He says: 'We're committed to a blend of the word and Spirit. Terry Virgo did a seminar specifically on the scriptural background to what is happening and we sought to help people understand the things that were happening round them.' He noted that scores of people among the 13,000 or more attending gave their lives to Christ.

The Stoneleigh Bible week also saw a new development in that the leaders sought to recognise that sometimes it was appropriate for a meeting to carry on, even if some were possibly being touched by God. One hundred and fifty young people were helped out of a meeting so that the other 850 could hear the sermon. In one New Frontiers church they started to provide a room where those who had received a 'touch' during a quiet part of a meeting could retire and receive prayer.

The faithful at Stoneleigh sang of 'days of heaven' but there were those in the world who were not convinced. The

Daily Mail returned to the 'Toronto' story after the appearance of former topless model Samantha Fox at the Greenbelt Christian Arts Festival. She had made a profession of faith after attending the Holy Trinity Brompton Alpha course. This course, which has been attended by scores of non-Christians, offers a fifteen-session introduction to Christianity. The newspapers had also noted that people were queuing to get into the church, this despite it being August, traditionally a slow month for HTB.

Daily Mail writer Geoffrey Levy was distinctly underwhelmed by the animal noises made by some (more about these in a later chapter). He stressed that 'the large number of Anglican churches showing interest in the phenomenon, and the informal charismatic style of worship, is creating anxiety in some conventional quarters that the Church of England may suffer from Toronto blessing "entryism" in much the same way as the Labour Party had to fight off the internal influence of communism.

'Officially, the Church of England says it is not worried. "We have no fears whatsoever of a takeover," said an official loftily. "If the happenings are not a case of following the crowd or mass hysteria, then it is a great sign of renewal. Why should we fear being taken over by the Holy Spirit? That would be great."'

Levy wheeled in a psychologist to explain what it was all about. '. . .Dr Dorothy Rowe puts the mass event down to peer pressure. "One starts and others feel obliged to join in in case it could mean that God is not talking to them".

'She puts the shaking down to the physiological charge of the excitement causing a massive release of adrenaline, and the belly laughter to its "social contagiousness in a situation where you are meant to be happy for having found God".'

The next day renowned political Conservative, high Anglican and Evangelical-baiter Paul Johnson waxed lyrical in the *Mail on Saturday* (3rd September 1994). He described the 'Toronto blessing' as 'charismatic religious hysteria' and over-religious behaviour as 'disquieting, embarrassing and repellent'. Revivalism, he warned, could turn into a 'devastating Frankenstein monster'. He felt that the established church was not doing its job and that charismatics were filling the vacuum. Surely the revivals of the past had been long forgotten?

He was worried, nevertheless. Alarmed friends of his argued that revivalism helped spark the independence of mind that led the Americans to break away from Britain, or the North to fight with the South over slavery. And wasn't it revivalists behind the prohibition movement? And didn't prohibition give organised crime a foothold in the States?

What we need, he informed us, is the religion of St Augustine, St Francis and Thomas More, 'the calm, reasoned, beautiful and uplifting system of Judeo-Christianity'. That, it seems, together with religious education in schools, is what will save the nation.

History is hardly on Johnson's side. Many would argue that Methodist revivalism helped prevent atheistic French-style political radicalism engulf Britain in the eighteenth century. Moravian Quakers and Methodists helped Wilberforce have the slave trade abolished. Shaftesbury reformed the factories and the penal system. The ultra-revivalist Salvation Army became one of the largest providers of voluntary social welfare facilities in the country.

Whatever misgivings the mainstream media may have been having, those who have been immersed in revival-style spirituality for several months are quite clear about its benefits.

The King's Church in Penzance, who have been experiencing the weeping and laughing phenomena since late 1993, after an elder visited a Rodney Howard-Browne meeting, are able to assess the longer-term fruit of the current renewal. 'We have seen people whom we have counselled for years changed almost overnight,' said church leader Ron Stringer. 'The left hand of biblical counselling has been complemented by the right hand of God's power. People who were full of fear or self-imposed restrictions have changed. They're not like they were eight months ago.'

This is clearly more than a flash in the spiritual pan.

4

A Broken-Hearted People

Some who observed the phenomena sweeping literally hundreds of churches, were not impressed.

The *Evangelical Times* (September 1994), a bastion of reformed, Calvinistic evangelicalism retold some stories from the newspapers. (So many critics do, seemingly lacking the courage or integrity to go to a meeting and see for themselves.)

Their writer Geoff Thomas had a question:

> We must ask what would be left in some contemporary meetings if all the protracted singing, hand-waving, altar calls, laying on of hands, fallings, slayings in the Spirit, glossolalia, and spontaneous speakings were ended by a man of God? Is there any heart once this husk is removed? But the heart is the mighty work of God in many, convicting, illuminating, regenerating and instructing by the Word preached with the Holy Ghost sent down from heaven. It is that for which we still watch and pray. Until that time it matters little to us being dubbed. . . 'anti-revival'. . .
>
> Our conviction is that there has never been a time when there was so much paraphernalia of a religious awakening with scarcely a trace of an awakening itself.

Is he right? How serious are those involved about sin and repentance? One of the major concerns of Clifford Hill, editor of *Prophecy Today* was the fact that he had consistently prophesied that revival would only come with repentance:

> That is why we continue to say through this ministry that God will not pour out his Holy Spirit upon an unholy people who are running after the ways of the world. Only when we seek the face of the Lord in humility, confessing our sins and asking his forgiveness for our share of the responsibility for the state of the world, will there be a breakthrough. . .

He goes on to analyse some of the phenomena which he regards with some alarm and ponders on both good and bad reports he has heard.

How should those involved respond to the severe negativism of Thomas and the probing questions of Hill? Is the charismatic/Pentecostal wing of the worldwide church on a spiritual thrill-seeking spree, or is there genuine depth? Let's now take a look at the actual experience of many of the churches involved and the statements of key leaders, as well as reflecting on the spiritual pilgrimage of one church – the Sunderland Christian Centre.

A spirit of repentance

From the very start there has been a note of repentance in the testimony of many churches and individuals. Queen's Road Baptist, one of the first churches to be touched, traces its renewal to personal and corporate repentance and a strong sense of the judgement of God at the 7th May Sunday-evening meeting.

Cobham-based church leader Gerald Coates remarked in the late summer that the renewal at his Pioneer People church had been characterised more by weeping than laughing. He had told *The Daily Telegraph* that he had been inundated with phone calls and information about individuals repenting and putting old grievances right. He also noted that people were talking of conviction of sin and the fear of the Lord among his congregation.

Writing in the October edition of *Alpha* magazine Coates reflected:

> Holy joy is only holy when matched by holy living. I don't mean static perfection. . . God has made full provision allowing us to turn (repent), confess, receive forgiveness and receive the kiss of God's presence.
>
> Holiness has to do with humility, being conscious of serving God, ensuring that his will and not ours is pursued. It also means confessing our sins as well as our faults to God and to one another as the Scriptures teach. It is because we are set apart for God that we are concerned with fulfilling the ordinary duties of life, going the 'extra mile' in service and relationships, and – most importantly – owning up when we get things wrong.
>
> . . . Whenever God moves by his Spirit, whatever the fun-filled manifestations, there is a soberness which accompanies much of the rest of our activity.

For Colin Dye, the senior Pastor of Britain's largest church, Kensington Temple (KT), repentance was at the core of his new encounter with God. He had been prayed for on Good Friday by an American, Frances Hunter. He had fallen, laughing onto the platform in full view of the congregation and despite five efforts to get up he couldn't. He comments, 'A new anointing came upon me and since then I have found a new freshness in my spiritual walk, with a fresh revelation from Scripture, and a new level of healing and anointing.'

KT's 5,000-strong congregation did not immediately plunge into the flood of renewal that was even then lapping at the doors of several other London churches. The phenomena associated with the 'blessing' were not unknown at KT, but Colin felt strongly that they should wait. He told readers of *City News* 'I knew that if the Lord was going to move in KT we had to set aside time.' He was keen to ensure that the whole of the church received from God and therefore

rescheduled all the meetings for September. He also testifies
that God was dealing with him. He told the congregation on
Sunday 4th September that God had brought him through a
time of repentance and caused him to address specific issues
in his own life.

Terry Virgo of New Frontiers also affirmed the importance of holiness. He told readers of *Frontline*, 'Many are
weeping their way in repentance to God to renew their walk
with him and are far more diligently guarding their lifestyle
so as not to grieve the Holy Spirit.'

For one Norfolk-based Christian this meant confession to
a church member that the attitudes that underlay his vigorous driving needed to be renewed, as they betrayed a deeper
rebellion.

David Campbell, minister of one Elim church told *Direction* magazine of the evening of repentance that he had
observed during his visit to the Toronto Airport Vineyard.

> On one of the evenings one of the local people spoke about con-
> fessing sins. All the men were encouraged to talk to someone
> else and, in the honesty and openness that followed, many of
> them were confessing to all kinds of sins, such as adultery,
> homosexuality and being hooked on pornography. There fol-
> lowed a time of deep cleansing and about half the people
> present ended up lying on their backs on the floor, some for two
> or three hours.

Bishop David Pytches of St Andrew's Chorleywood told a
Focus '94 audience that repentance is important, but the
heart that would experience it was one in love with or in
union with Christ:

> In Matthew 7:19-20 Jesus says, 'Every tree that does not bear
> good fruit is cut down and thrown into the fire. Thus by their
> fruit you will recognise them.' It doesn't say 'by their phenom-
> ena' but 'by their fruit' you will recognise them.
>   John the Baptist addressed the Pharisees and said to them:

'Produce fruit in keeping with repentance.' This repentance element is a very important thing. Repentance isn't always just turning away from adultery and murder and some of these more horrific kinds of sin. Repentance is putting things right – getting back into a right relationship with God. It is a change of attitude and mind and we are seeing a lot of that in St Andrew's.

I think when this refreshing moves out into the world and we see a lot of worldly people coming to Christ, we will see a lot more repentance. Some people say that when everyone begins to repent then we'll see revival. I believe when people begin to get revived, we should see some repentance.

We should not be earnestly striving to manifest strange and often amusing phenomena. Neither should we struggle about the fruit we are producing. The branch is not looking to the end of the branch to see what bunches are being produced there. The branch is meant to be focusing on union with Christ – this is where the abiding connects up with the anointing. The vital thing is that you and I abide.

Losing that relationship with Christ can rob us of our tender-heartedness. Brendon Munro, a North London Pentecostal pastor speaking of his experience in the spring and summer of 1994, testifies of how deeply God had searched him and his attitudes.

But my personal walk with Jesus has been wonderfully rejuvenated. It's as if my first love has returned, and the passion to know Jesus more and more is burning deep within. I have shed countless tears in the last couple of months as the Holy Spirit has gently led me in repentance. There have been tears for not having sought him so intensely in the past; for having lost my first love; and many tears of joy as waves of his love have broken afresh upon my life. I suddenly realised the irony of me, a Pentecostal minister, attending an Anglican prayer meeting to receive a fresh touch of the Holy Spirit! That called for repentance from spiritual pride. At another meeting with Anglican leaders to which I had been so warmly invited, I was stunned at the power of the praise and worship. Singing in the Spirit and wonderful prophetic words followed most blessed worship. I then found myself repenting of an elitist attitude – who was I to think that we Pentecostals had it all?

Then there was the realisation of just how often I had stood afar off, criticising and analysing any moves of God, never entering in. Sure, there are always some things a little untoward when God is moving powerfully; different people react in different ways and, yes, sometimes a bit of the flesh creeps in. But I had allowed the 'little foxes' to 'spoil the vine', and often missed the heart of what God was doing. So that was another area for repentance. I felt as if the Lord was spiritually spring-cleaning me on the inside, and it felt good.

Keri Jones, writing in *Restoration Truth* (Summer 1994) was quite clear that God was desiring holy lives as a result of this fresh outpouring:

The Lord is re-emphasising that his word is to be obeyed. Through obedience we are finding that his ways are pleasant and his paths are peaceful. Under the leading of the Holy Spirit, to walk in the ways of the Lord is not difficult. His commands are not burdensome. Let us meditate day and night in his word and so find success.

Maintain an attitude of repentance. During these times of refreshing, repentance is re-emerging as a foundation of Christian life and experience. Wrong attitudes, thought patterns, hurts and inner conditions of the heart are being removed by a swift operation of the Spirit.

Repentance is not confined to the beginning of our walk with Jesus. It evidences itself again and again as we continue to walk with the Lord. Today, repentance is proving to be for many the door to the healing process, producing a quality of life with no regrets.

The Sunderland story

God has dealt with churches and individuals in many and varied ways. The story of the Sunderland Christian Centre is perhaps typical of many, although I believe it has many unique features.

The church is an Assemblies of God church, planted in Sunderland nine years ago by Bethshan Tabernacle in Newcastle. The church grew rapidly and its members felt it right to erect a new building in the heart of an inner-city urban area. Several sold their houses and brought cheaper ones, using the profit to provide the money that would convince the bank to lend them the rest.

The church, capable of holding 800, is surrounded by a ten-feet-high fence to deter vandals, and following several attacks all the windows are now made of brick-resistant bullet-proof glass.

The church grew to 400 members by 1994 under the leadership of Ken and Lois Gott. Ken entered the ministry in his thirties after a successful early career as a fingerprint expert. Lois is the daughter of Herbert Harrison, who was for thirty-eight years the Minister of the Bethshan Church in Newcastle. He had been present when the ministry of Pentecostal pioneer Smith Wigglesworth was at his peak.

Ken and Lois were particularly aware of the Holy Spirit heritage of Sunderland. The British Pentecostal movement traces some of its roots to the 1907 revival in Sunderland under the ministry of T.B. Barratt and Alexander Boddy.

Things were looking good for the church. Ken felt he had a good team around him, a planned church plant was progressing towards its October launch. In July he received a phone call from Wes Richards, a pastor in Slough. Wes asked him if he was aware of what was happening at Holy Trinity Brompton (HTB). Wes said that he felt Ken should attend a leaders' meeting at HTB the following day.

Ken, with his thirty-nine years of Pentecostal tradition, sat and listened as Bishop David Pytches advised the leaders how to deal with this new outpouring of the Spirit. A row of Pentecostals at the back hadn't experienced this new 'blessing'. They sat and watched, slightly bemused, but sensing that God was in the place. One of them said, 'We need to go down the front and humble ourselves as Pentecostals and get the Anglican Bishop to pray for us.'

Pytches prayed a 'quiet, un-Pentecostal prayer' and said, 'Holy Spirit, these men need you, they desire you, come now and bless them.' Immediately 'all five of us were on the floor, laughing our heads off. It was the first time ever that this had happened to me – this went on for about ninety minutes.'

Pytches also prayed for them individually. They left changed. Ken reflects, 'It was like the burden and the pressure of that mundane, routine, rut-like experience we had been in had been lifted.'

The following Sunday night a hundred people gathered in the upstairs room at the church and many were touched with 'holy joy' after Ken shared from the word. 'There were people laughing that night who needed to laugh.'

A pattern of Sunday night 'seeking' meetings was established. Then Herbert Harrison suggested that Ken and Lois should visit Toronto. Ken had also been feeling this but was reluctant to use the church's general fund, given their mortgage commitments and other responsibilities.

Herbert told the congregation of his belief that Ken and Lois should go and felt that they shared his view. The congregation already gave an average of £3,000 or more every week, but on the morning that a second offering was taken, a further £3,500 was given, enabling Ken and Lois and the church youth leader to go to Toronto and to bless several others while they were there.

On the first night in Toronto (6th August) the couple received prayer. They and John Arnott had a mutual friend and John was keen to meet them in case he didn't have the opportunity on the Sunday. Before leaving for a rally he prayed for them in a corridor of the church. . . Lois was overcome with laughter. Ken had a vision of fires of revival all over the North of England.

The next day in the morning service Ken told the congregation: 'Just as Alexander Boddy travelled to Wales to see revival and bring it back to Sunderland, I am in Toronto to taste revival and refreshing and take it back with me.'

John Arnott and a Vineyard leader prayed with Ken and Lois again and they both fell to the ground. Lois testified of significant inner healing that morning. In the afternoon they received a significant prophecy about reaping the harvest. Part of the prophecy tied in with a dream that Lois had had eight years previously. There were many tears shed that afternoon.

On their return to Sunderland Ken stood to preach. He and Lois had agreed on the plane that they would not talk about the physical phenomena, so as to avoid any possibility that they were 'suggesting' anything to the congregation. 'I didn't want imitation, I wanted a visitation.'

Ken struggled to remain standing as he preached on his first morning back, but as he prayed for people he saw many of the same phenomena he had witnessed in Canada. 'I knew it could only be God.'

The church met every night the following week with over 150 people gathering nightly. Ken anticipated that they might do this for two weeks before his own congregation became 'saturated'. They didn't advertise the meetings, but soon visitors started to flock in and over 400 were attending – up to 600 on some nights. People were travelling in from a seventy-mile radius.

The church met nightly until the end of October, with a night off on Monday. In November they moved to four nights a week and a monthly rally. They had 'no big-name speakers – the people are coming for Jesus'.

'It's important that, bearing in mind God's blessing on us as a "refreshment centre", we keep our vision of local church life,' reflects Ken. 'We needed, after our initial twelve weeks of intensity, to trim down, so that there was room for local church life to continue.'

They also decided to make it clear that there would be a

special emphasis on Bible study in the continuing Thursday night meetings.

As the meetings progressed through September huge crowds attended on the evening following a special ladies' conference during the day. One of the speakers had been Carol Carnacki, a former drug addict and occultist. Ken reports: 'It was almost as if God spoke into my heart and said "How many Carol Carnackis are out there?" "Hundreds?" I suggested. "Thousands," God seemed to be saying. "I'm refreshing you, enjoy it, but it's for a purpose." I called the people to agree with me that when God commissioned us we would go to the world, recognising that God refreshed the church for the world. We've got to go out to the world with love and mercy, not just evangelistic programmes that look for numbers.'

Ken, speaking to me in September, painted the broad brush strokes of what God had done. Lois, his wife and co-worker, told me of the poignant stories of how God had touched individual lives.

Soon after Ken had returned from Holy Trinity Brompton they had a leaders' meeting. 'We sat, and one after the other various people went to the microphone. One lady said, "I know the impression you all have of me, that everything is together. It's just a front to cover up my insecurity. I know I appear busy, but it covers the fact that I feel that in my Christian walk I've never really felt that I had victory. God has shown me my heart and I confess it before you."

'Then one of the male leaders stood. "I need a prayer life. God has convicted me that I don't even pray. Will you all forgive me?"'

The previous Sunday morning God had moved after a reminder that God wasn't giving his Holy Spirit so that the church would have a reputation for power, but so that the people might love one another. About 95% of the congregation came to the front, many weeping as they asked the Lord to let them be people with the right motives and with hearts that didn't crave power or exercise favouritism.

Ken was preaching elsewhere that morning. Lois was surprised at the next development. 'A man began to shout "Jesus have mercy upon me." Some began to wail and weep very loudly and some were caught up in laughter. Some fell – nobody had touched them.' Lois was not totally at ease. She had never experienced a morning like it. She returned home and confided in a friend, 'I can't control it.'

'You can't control God,' her friend corrected her. 'Let God be God.'

Lois continues: 'As God has continued to touch us, he has been working on our hearts. Just as when gold is refined the dross rises to the surface, so we've been seeing interior change in people.'

One man from a Brethren background stood at the back of the church, wary about all that was happening. As the congregation sang 'How Great Thou Art' he felt God say, 'I'm going to show you how great I am.' He fell to the floor and couldn't get up. He had never had a vision in his life, but he saw in his mind's eye a mist covering the whole congregation, and a huge figure bent in the apex of the church. God told him he was concerned about the pride of his heart and spiritual pride. He half crawled to the front, weeping. He confessed the fact that he had controlled his church and he pledged to let God have the church back. Several other ministers came forward and made similar confessions.

On another occasion a doctor preached on spiritual eyesight. Many, he said, saw well with the eye of understanding, but the eye of the heart had 'lazy' muscles. Perhaps, he continued, God was doing things we didn't fully understand, covering the 'understanding eye' to cause us to use the eye of the heart and restore it to full strength.

A pastor visiting the church, who had confessed already to his own need for a fresh touch from God, crawled, weeping to the pulpit. He told 550 people, 'I haven't got that heart and I need it.' Several other pastors came forward and asked

God to give them a new heart for him.

Ken and Lois received a phone call from another church leader whose youth group had attended meetings at the Sunderland Christian Centre. He had been very worried about the young people for some time because of their attitude and behaviour. He himself wasn't entirely sure what he thought about the current 'time of refreshing', but the young people had returned transformed – throwing themselves into the worship, no longer skulking in the back row. The change was so dramatic they had to have an elders' meeting to discuss how the church could respond positively. The church started three extra meetings.

Another pastor, a Pentecostal, wary of all that was happening attended the midweek pastors' meeting. He fell down and felt God told him that he didn't love his congregation, and that God wanted him to truly love them and give himself to them. He went to his church the following Sunday, and as he served communion he and several others fell under the power of God. The fruit of it was that several relationships were put right that morning.

Suzette Hattingh, a personal friend of the Gotts who works with Reinhard Bonnke, spearheading the intercession that takes place before his crusades, has visited the Airport Vineyard and the Sunderland Christian Centre. 'In Toronto God took care of my pride, in Sunderland God broke my heart. People's hearts are being changed. I felt more aware of God's presence last night in the meeting than the manifestations that were taking place. I've found the worship and the focus on Jesus very strong here.'

One family has been totally transformed. The husband was depressed and contemplating suicide, the wife considering leaving him because of the misery he caused her and the children. He was touched by God and was physically weakened for days. 'He realised that in the midst of fear of rejection by the family, he was rejecting them first and lashing out. God dealt with him. The whole family say he's like a new man, and there's a new joy in his life. He's well known and many are noticing.'

One lady, who had always been loved by her family, but received little affection, saw while on the floor a picture of a no-entry sign. She asked God what it meant and felt he said, 'That's the entrance to your heart.'

All of these insights and stories are perhaps only a fore-taste. John Wimber in a leadership letter has said, 'People have asked me what I think the next step may be. I've said that at some point in time we must give a call to full-scale repentance undergirded by deep and heartfelt contrition. Changed lives and the fruit of true repentance will result.'

5

The Toronto Connection

'British Airways flight number 092 took off from Toronto Airport on Thursday evening just as the Holy Spirit was landing on a small building a hundred yards from the end of the runway.'

Describing the Toronto Airport Vineyard as the 'place to be' in the world of charismatic evangelicalism, the *The Sunday Telegraph* of the 19th June 1994 told its several million readers that a revival of evangelism was sweeping around the world from the church.

The fresh spiritual fire had been sparked by a South African evangelist, an Argentinian pastor and this small church. For many, touched by God prior to their visit, the Toronto Vineyard was not the place they rediscovered the power of the Spirit, but a place where they learned to pursue God and how to help others pursue him.

By the end of September, some 90,000 had attended meetings in the church, with perhaps as many as 40,000 being 'first timers' from the USA, Egypt, England, Cambodia, Germany, Switzerland, Ireland and dozens of other countries, who had flown in to 'catch the fire'.

The Airport Vineyard, in human terms, was not an auspicious place for a renewal or revival to be birthed. Only 350 people from the sprawling five million population of the Greater Toronto area attended the church, which met in the end block of a warehouse/office complex. The pastor John Arnott and his wife Carol were a happily married couple, but both had known the break-up of their previous marriages.

Local churches were hostile to their ministry, with one Ontario pastor issuing a leaflet on 'How to keep the Vineyard out of your vineyard'. (He subsequently repented in a pastors' meeting at the Toronto church.)

The church had links with a well-known healing and deliverance ministry, which many in the mainstream charismatic/Pentecostal movement in Britain consider to be extreme. The pastor was also a long-time friend of Benny Hinn who, until his very public renunciation of several of their key doctrines in an interview with *Charisma* magazine, had been a high-profile speaker and healing evangelist associated with the word of faith movement. This brand of teaching was under vigorous scrutiny within the charismatic and evangelical camps, initially because of its health-and-wealth emphasis, but latterly because of the promotion by some of a 'faith is a force' philosophy, the doctrine that Jesus died 'spiritually' in hell and the 'little gods' doctrine which argued that if our words conform with God's law, we can create reality, much as he did.

The Toronto Airport Vineyard definitely didn't hold to word-of-faith doctrines, but its leadership was friendly with some of the most controversial figures in the worldwide charismatic movement.

If it had been left to you and me we wouldn't necessarily have chosen this as a 'refreshment centre' for God's people and a catalyst for potential revival. And why on the face of it would God choose a Canadian city? Airport Vineyard pastor Marc Dupont thinks he knows why. 'Toronto is, according to the United Nations, the most ethnically diverse city in the world. It's a great city for something to be birthed in because it can be a sending out place.'

At the core of the story of how the Toronto Airport became the church which sparked what the media dubbed 'the Toronto blessing', is the personal spiritual pilgrimage of John and Carol Arnott.

Following their marriage in 1979 they undertook a business trip to Indonesia in 1980. They had the opportunity to preach and share and saw a significant response. The thought that they might be more than Christian business people, and could actually help pioneer, was rekindled and in 1981 they helped establish a church in Stratford, Ontario.

In 1986 this new church affiliated itself with the growing Vineyard movement and John eventually became an area pastoral co-ordinator for the southern Ontario region. The church grew, and the Arnotts felt called to a new challenge.

In 1988 they pioneered the Toronto Airport Vineyard and eventually moved there in 1992. The church numbered 350 people by late 1993.

The church reflected the Arnotts' wariness of any kind of 'hit-and-run' ministry model. In John's words, when people got saved they worked to help 'make it stick'. They emphasised repentance, deliverance and inner healing and started to train up a seventy-strong ministry team to help people through the often lengthy period when their previously shattered lives were reconstructed.

John was not entirely happy: 'Because this type of ministry is tedious and time-consuming, you can end up with a "big devil" and a "little God".' A breakthrough came when he attended a Benny Hinn meeting where a deaf person heard and several others were healed. He was reminded afresh that he worshipped a big God, who was more than capable of breaking Satan's power in a person's life.

Looking to his own spiritual heritage John believed there were answers to this imbalance. He believed that a powerful encounter with the Holy Spirit could provide the breakthrough. 'I knew that it took the anointing to really set people free. We'd seen it in Kathryn Kuhlman's ministry and that totally ruined us for settling for more traditional ministry models.'

Those familiar with the Vineyard movement will know that the idea of a 'power encounter' would not jar with their ministry ethos. Like his Vineyard associates, however, John was committed to pastoral practices that sought to take seriously the priesthood of all believers. He knew some individuals who were 'mighty men' but he wanted to help spiritually nurture a mighty people. As he spent time with God he felt prompted to spend time with people who seemed anointed by God to move powerfully in the gifts of the Spirit.

God also said: 'I want your mornings.' The Arnotts decided to change the way they organised their daily lives and for eighteen months in 1992 and 1993 they set aside every morning for personal prayer, worship and reading of the word.

They were feeding their spiritual fire, but John wasn't always ready to receive from God. He spent time with Benny Hinn, and was prayed for in June 1993 by Rodney Howard-Browne. As John remembers it: 'Two hundred and forty-eight people fell down, but I was still standing. My mind on these occasions slips into analysis and control.'

In November 1993 John and Carol attended a conference in Argentina. This conference was hosted by leading Argentinian Christian figures such as Ed Silvoso, Hector Jiminez and Omar Cabbarra, and was attended primarily by North American pastors. The pastors were encouraged to seek the face of God, not just the working of his hand, but some were to receive a new empowerment nevertheless.

It was here that John met and was prayed for by Claudio Freidzon. Like Arnott, Freidzon had been on a personal spiritual journey. He had sought to develop a deeper intimacy with God, and he had also received an 'impartation' of spiritual anointing from both Benny Hinn and Rodney Howard-Browne.

The troubled Arnott, still battling with his own spiritual formalism, was asked by Freidzon if he wanted this new empowerment, and if so to 'take it'. Arnott felt the Lord was prompting him. 'For goodness sake will you take this?' He did and testified to significant healing and restoration as he surrendered to God.

He then travelled to Palm Springs to a meeting of the Vineyard churches' national board and council. Vineyard leader, John Wimber, shared his belief that God had prompted him repeatedly that this was a time of new beginnings, and that God wanted to stir up the church.

In this atmosphere of spiritual anticipation, John also met Happy Leman, another Vineyard leader who told him of the powerful renewal and refreshment that Randy Clark, pastor of the St Louis Vineyard had experienced after attending a Howard-Browne meeting. John contacted him and asked him to come and speak at a four-day series of meetings for the southern Ontario churches. The meetings, which started on 20th January at the Airport Vineyard, astonished Arnott, despite his fervent faith and hope that God would move in revival power. 'Instead of ministering to several people as normal, it seemed as if the whole congregation had been touched.'

Arnott admits to a severe fear that if Clark went the blessing would settle back down to normal levels. He prevailed upon him to stay for another week and later flew Clark's wife up from St Louis for a further week. Clark was to visit the church intermittently several times until mid-March and again in August.

John, who had longed for a time when the church would meet every day, had read about the ministry of Billy Sunday and the Azusa Street revival of 1906 – which helped spawn the worldwide Pentecostal movement – and here it was happening now.

The vision of John and Carol Arnott had been reinforced by several prophecies. Airport pastor Marc Dupont had foreseen tremendous blessing in the southern Ontario region. A complete stranger had walked into the church offices and prophesied over John.

As this book goes to print the church continues to meet every night. Over the summer months numbers increased. In mid-October a *Catch the Fire* conference seemed likely to attract over 2,000 people. Over 3,000 church leaders had visited. It was conservatively estimated that 2,500 had rededicated their lives to Christ and that at least 300 had accepted Christ for the first time.

The impact began to rumble around the world. In the spring, Norman Moss of Queen's Road Baptist Church, Wimbledon, Alan Preston of Church of Christ the King, Brighton, Elli Mumford of the South West London Vineyard and Bishop David Pytches of St Andrew's Chorleywood visited Toronto. All four were to be pivotal in helping to encourage a hunger for and the release of a time of refreshing in the United Kingdom. By mid-June the mainstream press were writing stories.

So what was happening to people who fell to the floor after prayer? Was this merely an emotional, but ultimately shallow charismatic bless-me-up?

I travelled to Toronto in early August to see for myself. My initial response to news of the impact of Rodney Howard-Browne and the laughter among the followers of Claudio Freidzon was deep suspicion. I for one was hostile to the idea of any charismatic fad that promoted a 'pursuit of perpetual excitement' but didn't help promote a greater love for Jesus and real Christian maturity.

People in the UK were being touched as early as November/December 1993 through contact with Rodney Howard-Browne and various Argentinians. When it became clear that a Vineyard church and the New Frontiers network were being touched, I was intrigued. Both John Wimber and Terry Virgo, the respective leaders of these groups, had a reputation for being concerned with having a thoughtful faith. Evangelical scholars such as John White and Wayne Grudem, Charles Kraft and Jack Deere had been attracted to the Vineyard movement because of its moderate stance. Wimber was the antithesis of a wild American Pentecostal. Terry Virgo, speaking in Sheffield in 1990 to 1,000 charismatic leaders, had called for a 'return to the apostles' doctrine' (Acts 2:42), instead of the 'winds of doctrine' that buffeted the charismatic ship.

Before I left for Toronto I talked to Marc Dupont, one of the pastoral team at the Airport Vineyard, and discovered that he felt God had told him about ten days previously that he would have a meeting in London with a journalist and that it would be an important meeting. He then shared with me a prophetic word. He seemed to be aware of several aspects of the way I thought and ministered in public, although he vigorously discouraged me, prior to our praying together, from talking about my own personal ministry, in order that his perceptions about what God might be desiring to say to me would not be coloured by things I said.

I was both encouraged and alarmed by what he said, as change was forecast. As always I adopted a 'wait and see' attitude towards his prophecy.

Also in the days before the Toronto trip I attended two large meetings. At one I witnessed weeping, laughing and many prostrate on their faces before God. The next night was like a roller-coaster ride with emotions running high. The meeting was significantly interrupted by a 'roaring lion'. Being a visitor I could do little. My first inclination however was to go over and give some fairly terse and to-the-point counsel to the person involved. A vital sermon was being interrupted!

I arrived in Toronto and settled in the White Knight Motel, just a hundred yards from the church. It was basic, but convenient.

The following morning I wandered over to the church and began to get my bearings. The staff were affable, relaxed, casually dressed and non-religious. Stories of God moving in individual lives peppered their conversation, but they also had tales to tell about self-declared prophets and other amusing moments during the previous six months.

Crossing the main meeting room to get to the canteen I felt a definite sense that I was in a special place. The room is square, tastefully decorated in a relaxing green and holds about 500 in comfortable padded chairs. Huge fans in the roof give the room an icy edge until the people pour in for the meetings. I had experienced this 'feeling' before, sometimes in places where the spiritual spark had all but gone out, but where there had been great blessing over the years.

By 7.00 pm the room was full. I was jittery as the meeting began. There was a large group in from Kentucky. They periodically yelped and one of them yelled 'Big God!' whenever the phrase was used on the platform.

As the meeting progressed, some trembled, shook or jerked. We were proceeding towards the ministry time and, like many before me, I stood 'hugging the back wall' and observing. Some stood with arms flailing, others marched on the spot, others lay shaking. As pastor John Arnott walked around praying for people the word 'apprentice' came into my mind. I was mildly horrified. I was in two minds about all I was witnessing; why would I want to be an apprentice to the pastor?

The next day I attended the pastors' meeting where John Arnott talked openly and honestly of his spiritual pilgrimage. Guy Chevreau, a local pastor and historian of recent events, spoke on Jonathan Edwards' analysis of revival phenomena.

That night in the meeting I sat in the overflow. I was having a minor internal battle. During the worship and testimonies I had written down several encouraging things God had reminded me of. Looking out across the room I had also noticed a girl whose whole appearance said 'tender-hearted'. The phrase 'imagine what a tender-hearted generation could do' had come into my mind. I had drifted off into a detached reverie as several potential sermon points came to mind.

But I was wary of this state. I knew it well from previous experience. It often happens in meetings and is usually a prelude to me sharing some kind of prophetic or inspirational insight. That wasn't appropriate here and anyway, wasn't I here to observe and perhaps receive a touch from God?

I summoned up the courage to ask for prayer and suspended my bafflement at the sight of some of the twitching faithful. One woman who had testified, mentioned that her pastor husband never fell down. He sounded like my kind of man. I got him to pray for me. I stood there in some trepidation, my mind on full alert. Nothing happened.

Back in my hotel room that night I told the Lord that he would probably have to sneak up on me, as I tended to freeze in a prayer line.

As the week progressed I was prayed for several times and fell to the ground twice. I wasn't 'stricken' as some are, but felt my balance going and decided to stop resisting. I was not pushed by anybody at any time.

I met with Marc Dupont again for a meal and stood in a side office at the church as he prayed for me. I was aware that something was happening and felt slightly shaky as I walked back to the hotel room. Throughout the afternoon I felt waves of warmth and felt prompted to write down several key areas of interest that I often dwelt on in my own inner spiritual conversations. I thought that they were merely my own interests, but I was beginning to discover that some of what I was reflecting on, others were also preaching and writing about. Maybe the Holy Spirit was prompting me more than I thought.

I then interviewed John Arnott and he took me under his wing for the rest of the week, encouraging me to follow him round in the meetings and to understand the different nature of the encounter with God that many were having. I became his 'apprentice' for five days, catching people as they fell and praying for some. I was prayed for too and received specific encouragement from the words that were prayed over me.

I was still somewhat bemused but found myself working alongside the Kentucky people whose behaviour had so alarmed me on the first night. They were quite sane – if a little unusual in their spiritual expression.

But the week's most profound moment for me was still to come. We were praying for an English pastor, Ken Gott, on the Saturday night. I asked God to use him to set the 'fire of God across the North of England'. Ken is the pastor of the 400-strong Sunderland Christian Centre. He immediately saw a vision of fires breaking out across the northern terrain and shouted at the top of his voice, 'I can see it! I can see it!' I stepped back. This had never happened before when I prayed for someone!

The next day as John and Carol Arnott prayed for him again, Ken went into a trance-like state and began thrashing around. John asked him what was happening and Ken indicated that he was trying to get through a hedge. This hedge symbolised unhelpful traditions and expectations. As I sat and pondered where all this fitted into my theological grid I began to wonder what Ken would do when he saw through the hedge. The word 'harvest' and a mental image of a field of golden corn with Ken carrying bales of it, came to me. I shared this with him. It was then that his wife Lois began to weep.

Eight years before Lois and her mother had had the same dream about her soon-to-be-born baby. The dream concerned tragic circumstances at the birth. Sadly it all happened and the child was lost. Lois had also dreamed of leaving the hospital, apparently pregnant again, and standing in front of a field of wheat. Behind her husband she could see someone explaining what it meant, but she couldn't hear or see him properly.

Over the years she had had many prophetic words but none mentioned a field of wheat. In the months before Toronto she had received a word about being 'about to give birth'.

That morning, having been prayed for in the church, she had felt her fear of hospitals and death flow away, as she was touched by God with an understanding of what it would be like to dance around heaven. The residual emotional pain from the loss of her child began to dissolve. With this in mind, the falling into place of the last piece of her dream jigsaw prompted a waterfall of tears.

John Arnott looked across at me. 'You're shocked, aren't you?' I was. It's one thing to share a 'picture'. It's another discovering its part in an astonishing sequence of events.

I left Toronto Airport Vineyard different from when I arrived. I had not spent hours 'on the carpet'. But several things had happened to jolt me out of my self-doubt over whether I could genuinely hear from God. Marc Dupont's words, spoken to me several weeks before, about hearing from God in a very natural way and thinking it was me rather than him, had proved to be true.

I had also been close to tears several times, particularly when we were praying for people from other nations.

Intellectually I had been open to the idea that we might be on the verge of renewal and revival. Emotionally, and in that corner of the mind where healthy scepticism and cynical doubt are uneasy bedfellows, I had still been doubting. My visit to Toronto began to change that. The servant attitudes, the lack of hype, the wariness of being 'flaky', the diversity of ministry, the Christ-exalting worship, the passion for Jesus and a deeply moving sermon about the cross disarmed me.

I was one of thousands. Guy Chevreau, a local Toronto pastor and the author of *Catch the Fire* (the inside story of what has happened at the Airport Vineyard) turned up at the church on 1st February harbouring the suspicion that what was happening was 'very flaky'. He came 'just in case', describing himself as 'too desperate to be critical'. He was finding his local church situation less than straightforward. His wife was 'drunk' for forty-eight hours after the first meeting. The second time they attended Guy started to weep as he lay on the floor. 'I felt the insensitivity, resentment and bitterness in my life being lifted, and received a powerful re-commission for service to Christ.'

This new purpose was vital for Guy. Describing the outward phenomena as 'bells and whistles' he comments that if it was only that, and did not involve a new sense of purpose and commission, 'Then I've got a question.'

For some there are few or no outward phenomena; for others mighty miracles.

Marc Dupont, pastoral team member at the Airport church, has had a quiet revolution. 'I haven't fallen in the Spirit. I haven't shaken in the Spirit. I haven't laughed uncontrollably. I haven't been weeping in meetings. I haven't had anything happen to me overtly. On the other hand since mid-January, when I spent time alone with God and felt he spoke to me of his love for me, his hope for me, his friendship for me, I know that my own prayer life has been much more consistent than in the past.'

During my time at the Vineyard, I heard several people testify of healing from dyslexia and wheat allergies. The most poignant story however is that of Sarah. The following account is drawn from the church newsletter.

In October 1991 Sarah Lilleman, then thirteen years old, caught what her parents thought was the flu but which was in fact something much more debilitating. Her eyesight, congenitally very poor, further degenerated; her memory and cognitive abilities deteriorated. At Peel Memorial and Sick Children's Hospitals Sarah underwent extensive testing but no medical causes for her symptoms were detected. Admitted to hospital at that time, she remained there until March 1992. Sarah returned home in virtually the same condition as when she was admitted to the hospital.

As time went on, Sarah started to suffer loss of muscle control as well as loss of cognitive abilities. In October 1993 Sarah became like a vegetable, unable to walk, eat, swallow or even see. By January '94 she was transferred to Bloorview, a hospital for chronic care patients, for she needed the aid of a mini-hoist to be put to bed.

On February 27, 1994, Sarah's friend, Rachel Allalouf, came to the evening service of the Airport Vineyard where Randy Clark was speaking. After his message, Rachel received prayer. While she was on the floor resting in the Lord, she had a vision of being at a table in heaven with her two grandfathers and with Jesus. As the vision changed to a picture of a cross, Rachel heard Jesus ask her to go to the hospital the next day and pray for Sarah exactly as He had explained. The next day at the hospital Rachel and her father, Siman Allalouf, wheeled Sarah to a quiet place and began to pray. Sarah, unable to move, was in her special wheelchair described as a 'stretcher on wheels'. Sarah couldn't see or comprehend what was being said but she recognised the voices of her friends. As they prayed over the next two-and-a-half hours, Sarah began to cry, then shake. Her sight began to come back and her legs started to move. She slowly began to sit up on her own, and her previously uncontrollable drooling stopped. The joy of the Lord started to fill her and she kept saying 'I'm getting stronger and stronger!' Rachel was so convinced that Jesus was going to heal Sarah that she brought in a bag of dill pickle chips for her to eat. Over the next few days Sarah began walking and eating, even the chips, on her own! Her eyesight continued to improve. Word of Sarah's recovery quickly went around the hospital. A few days later, a woman at the front desk came up to Siman and Rachel and said, 'The power of Jesus is real, isn't it?' She was a believer and, as Siman reports, was thrilled that the Lord had come and visited with His healing power. She then asked them to pray for her alcoholic, unbelieving husband.

On April 22 1994, Sarah returned home from Bloorview Hospital. She had not been expected to ever leave the chronic care hospital. Sarah was able to attend the night service at Airport Vineyard with Rachel. That night, Rachel received a further word from the Lord: if Sarah would go to the front of the church and testify of what had happened, the Lord would continue to heal her eyes. This was a hard step for Sarah, because of her fear of people, but she did it because she trusted God.

Her whole family has undergone radical change and each is closer than ever to each other and to God. Sarah's mother brought a friend to the Vineyard meetings. Her friend entered as an unbeliever but left as a follower of Christ. Siman's unbelieving wife came to the meetings at Airport Vineyard and now has given her life to the Lord. Siman told an old friend of the miracle in Sarah's life. This friend then came to the meetings and gave his heart to Jesus. Siman concludes his report: 'We just want to give all the praise and glory to the Lord Jesus. We love Him with all of our hearts and nothing, absolutely nothing, is before Him. He is the Alpha and the Omega. Praise Yeshua!'

For others, the refreshment came in the midst of a desert time.

Brendon Munro, a London Pentecostal pastor, had already been having dealings with God before he arrived. 'I was hungry and thirsty for the Lord. After just ten years in full-time ministry I seemed to be in a dry and barren place, desperate for God to refresh and renew me. I had reached the end of myself.' He visited Holy Trinity Brompton, reflecting that it was ironic for a Pentecostal pastor to 'be visiting an Anglican church to receive prayer for a fresh touch of the Holy Spirit'.

His Toronto experience was meaningful.

The first person who prayed for me wore a brightly coloured badge that read 'Ministry Team Trainee'. I saw her coming and wondered whether I could quickly dodge her and stand in a spot where John Arnott or Randy Clark would find me. I wanted them to pray for me. I could almost see the hand of God scrawling graffiti on the wall of my heart – 'Pride Must Die'. Is my faith in the one who prays or the One who answers prayer?

So this dear lady prays for me and I start to sway. I lock my knees, tense my leg muscles. I'm waiting for God to hit me with a baseball bat. I'm almost defying him to knock me over in spite of myself. The hardness of my heart shocks me. How little I know of my heavenly Father. The lady counsels me. 'Why are you resisting?' she asks. I don't know. She's hardly touching me, but I'm convinced she's pushing. 'Don't push me,' I say. She continues to pray, this time standing well back. I stop resisting, stop locking my knees and tensing my leg muscles, and gently sink to the floor. I lie there feeling vulnerable, yet safe, soaking in the love of the Father.

As the week progresses, I put in more 'floor time'. On one occasion I'm lying at the front with about twenty other full-time ministers from overseas and I'm laughing. My sides are aching. I feel silly. I wonder what on earth my congregation would think of me if they could see me. Who cares! My religious dignity has just been siphoned off in the furnace of God's love. Like a child, I'm just enjoying the love and joy of my Father, my Saviour, my Lord and God.

As I'm lying there I realise that the experience itself, the experience of falling over and laughing, is actually not so important. But God has used these unusual experiences to get my attention, to challenge and change my attitudes. My heart has been enlarged. God is bigger than I thought, mightier than I imagined.

Some have been blessed in spite of their own personal preferences. Charismatic elder statesman Michael Harper visited the church in early August. Writing in the *Church of England Newspaper* (9th September 1994) he admits an initial scepticism about the 'Toronto blessing'. He visited the church during a twenty-four-hour stop-over in Toronto.

'What with tiredness, the heat, jetlag and unattractive music I was not in the best of moods when the meeting started.' Not familiar with the latest Vineyard songs, unimpressed with the band, underwhelmed by the length of the sermon, he found it hard to believe this was the new 'Azusa Street'.

'But from the moment I stepped inside the door I knew God was there, and the rest didn't really matter. . . What was clear to me from the first minute was that something extraordinary was happening, and that this was due not to human factors, but to the divine presence and power. . . There was a complete absence of hype.'

He notes the dedication of the people who minister in the church. Every evening ministry team members and worship bands from churches throughout southern Ontario gather to work alongside the Airport staff members.

'There was no showing off, no reports of how great their church and ministry were. A quite remarkable degree of self-effacement, surely another sign of the true work of the Holy Spirit. No one was boasting except in God and His mercy.'

He wasn't too happy with the laughing, that night's roaring lion, and the falling backwards, but couldn't help but feel it was 'basically good'.

The touch of God that many experience at the church had a profound effect on the Sojourn Church of Carrolton, Texas.

Pastor Terry Moore saw a fresh wave of life sweep the church after a group visited Toronto. A man who suffered with a great deal of hip pain found himself on the floor one night back in his home church. He became aware of a woman praying for him. She told him she had had a vision of a skeleton and that God was realigning his bones. 'I got up off the floor and the stiffness and pain were gone. I could tell that my back and hip area were in alignment. What a wonderful gift he gave me!'

Dave Keeler was profoundly touched in Toronto. He wept as he felt comforted by God through words of prophecy, and laughed and shook in other meetings. Reflecting on the whole experience he said, 'Physical manifestations of the presence of the Holy Spirit are a temporary experience. The most precious part of this whole experience has been a new closeness to the Lord that is ongoing. For the first time in over thirty-seven years as a believer, I have been able to enter into a conversation with the Lord. The sense of being loved and in a loving relationship with the Lord is overwhelming.'

For Ann Heckenlaibe there was divine weeding that needed to be done during her Toronto visit.

'At one point I heard that loving, still small voice of the

Lord say, "I am your Father, now I want you to extend my love to your earthly father." I wept a lot and during that time I was delivered from a lot of pain. . . Since all this has started the Lord has done a wonderful restoration of my relationship with my dad, unlike anything we ever had in the past.'

Angela Weir had a similar experience: 'He rains, then he weeds. During the services, the Lord has touched me with his joy and laughter and spoken to me through visions. This is what I call the rain. The rain seems to be causing "the weeds" that are lodged in my heart to surface. The Lord. . . is pulling them out as I choose to yield.'

Diane Lafving was touched by God at Sojourn. The congregation had literally run to the front to receive from God. 'As I fell back I began laughing. . . with the angels I could see in my spirit. They were laughing at how serious-to-death we had been about our walks with God. They were rejoicing over us that we were finally free from our prideful inhibitions. They were amused at how puny the demons were that had held us back, compared to the power of God. . . As God is my Helper, I will never wring my hands over the wiles of the enemy again. . . Since then, the peace in my heart about my family and his purpose in us has never left me. Even when my eyes see something unpleasant or ungodly, my spirit has been healed of fearing the future.'

The meetings in which these life-changing experiences took place conformed to a similar pattern. The congregation, most of which arrive an hour before the service, is led in worship for perhaps as long as an hour. The music is dominated by the songs of Graham Kendrick, Kevin Prosch, David Ruis and Brian Doerksen. In the 'sermons in song' that precede the actual sermon, the congregation is drawn again and again to the cross. 'We ask not for riches, but look to the cross,' testifies Prosch in 'Show Your Power'. 'Amazing Love, O what sacrifice' is the cry of Kendrick.

On Thursday 4th August, the worship leader introduced two hymns, 'Crown Him with Many Crowns' and 'Holy,

Holy, Holy, Lord God Almighty'. In the pauses between the verses the congregation shouted and cheered its affirmation of the God-exalting lyrics. It's difficult to convey just how exultant the people were that evening, but I've never heard cheering during hymns before.

After the worship the leader of the meeting will invite people touched by God on previous nights to testify. It can be hard to stay composed even at this point of the service. A Cambodian pastor testifies of how he had been one of only three people who survived the massacre of over 600 in his village. This man who has spent years in jail has helped to start ten churches in recent years.

A father weeps as he tells of the healing of his son's asthma and his daughter's dyslexia. And then they receive more prayer as others with similar illnesses, needs or callings are invited to receive prayer.

The sermon follows. One night in early August, John Arnott spoke of the party that God's rejoicing people would have in his presence. He reminded the congregation of the price that Christ had paid so that we might know freedom from sin and rebellion. People wept as he spoke of Christ's suffering.

At the end of every sermon those who are not Christians, or who are backslidden, are invited to receive Christ. After prayer they are led away to a side room and given a new-believer pack and details of a New Life class. Then the rest of the congregation is invited to receive prayer. The chairs are stacked and the ministry team wander around the congregation, praying for people, as the worship band plays.

In order to maintain accountability in ministry the church discourages 'freelance' praying. The ministry team are drawn from Vineyard churches in the area, or from trusted leaders from other churches, and can be identified by their red and yellow badges. This helps stop cranks from infiltrating the ministry times and also helps the leaders from all around the world to relax. Even if they want to pray for people they are initially discouraged until they have had time to understand what is happening and to receive themselves.

At 10.00 pm the café opens and people begin slowly to leave. Many however will remain in the church receiving ministry and prayer until after midnight. Some visit the café and then return to the main meeting room.

The British can often be seen fellowshipping in the café. You don't need a word of knowledge to discern who they are. The women have less make-up and have styled hair rather than perms. The men are smaller than their Canadian/American counter-parts.

In the midst of all this fervent spiritual activity the Airport Vineyard tries to maintain something of its identity as a local church. The July 1994 church newsletter notes: 'We are trying to get our regular church activities back on track; namely Kinship [the British equivalent would be a home group], Recovery Groups and Leadership training. . . Ministry Team Training will be done "on the job" with occasional extra group sessions. We also have many new people to integrate into our church family. . . We definitely have growing pains, but we are deeply grateful to the Lord for honouring us with His presence in such wonderful ways.'

Sometimes the church motto, 'Walk in God's Love, and then Give it Away' has been tested. Youth pastor Brian West spoke to the Sunday congregation on 31st July, and grasped the nettle. He admitted that after the first three months he was tired and wished some nights that the congregation would 'go to their hotel rooms: the Holy Spirit is there too'. He changed his perspective when he felt God say to him, 'Would you like me to stop this because of your attitude?' He encouraged the congregation to avoid bitterness, criticism or judgement. The bitterness problem, he noted laughingly, often related to the problems of finding a parking space. He identified the feeling of some that they 'had lost their church' but affirmed that they liked the new one.

The brokenness that characterises the life and former circumstances of many of the congregation means that Brian's honest but nevertheless positive attitude is the norm.

Perhaps God has been able to use them all because hype is an anathema. They admit that the renewal meetings have hit the twelve-group home-meeting structure. Despite positive reactions from the young people, the eleven-to-fourteen-year-olds don't think what's happening is 'cool'. With so many visitors, the locals now have name tags on Sunday morning to help maintain some local identity.

What emerges is that in many ways the Airport Vineyard is a church like yours and mine. It's not perfect, but God has used it.

Will they move on into a revival that sees many unconverted people drawn to Christ and the Toronto area shaken by the power of God? John Arnott certainly yearns for that, but has held back on a more vigorous thrust in the short term because he felt God told him that he wanted to show his people his love for a while longer. John told the Sojourn church magazine, 'We need to fall in love with Jesus again, because people in love will get the job done. Have you ever noticed that people in love don't get tired? . . .our walk with God is all about romance, about receiving God's love and then pouring it on others.'

Pastoral team member Marc Dupont echoes John: 'As we start getting filled with that perfect love, then fear of rejection, fear of failure and fear of being laughed at begin to lose their control over us and we are more free to do evangelism, more free to talk to our neighbour, more free to pray for the lady down the street who's got cancer, more free to talk to someone in the office that we know is anti-Christian but God said talk to them. I believe that this will lead to major, major revival in the western world nations. . . This is a time of restoration in the body of Christ similar to the time of John the Baptist's ministry prior to the coming of the Messiah.

'Churches that choose to respond now are going to experience first fruits in terms of people getting saved and healed.'

May it be so.

6

Rodney Howard-Browne

As one puts together the jigsaw of the 1993/94 renewal a key piece at the centre of the picture is Rodney Howard-Browne, a South African-born evangelist.

His meetings are known for their 'holy joy', and his name occurs in any discussion of Toronto Airport Vineyard 'fire-lighter' Randy Clark, Argentinian pioneer Claudio Freidzon, and British pastors such as Bryn Jones (Covenant Ministries) and Terry Virgo (New Frontiers).

Rodney was born on 12th June 1961 in Port Elizabeth, South Africa, to devout Pentecostal parents. He witnessed early miracles in the life of his mother and father and took particular note of their commitment to prayer. He committed his life to Christ at the age of five and had a formative experience of the Holy Spirit as an eight-year-old.

In July 1979 he sought God for a fresh manifestation of himself. 'I cried out to God in sheer desperation. . . I was hungry. He told me that I had to hunger and thirst. At first I said to him "Why don't you just give it to me? I have served you all my life. I have been a good boy. I haven't done this, I haven't done that, as others have. God, I deserve it."

'He said, "I'm not a respecter of persons. You come the same way everyone else does. You come in faith and you get hungry and you desire it. Then I'll give it to you."'

Rodney persevered and 'suddenly the fire of God fell on

me. His power burned in my body and stayed like that for three whole days. I thought I was going to die.'

Soon the 'on-fire' Rodney is asking God, 'Please lift it off me so that I can bear it.' He was to feel something of the fire feeling for a further two weeks.

Rodney joined a Christian music group in 1980, but was diplomatically silent about his fiery Pentecostal beliefs. One night in a Methodist church another band member asked for prayer for healing. Rodney felt power go through him and the girl fell to the floor. The rest of the team walked in and he prayed for them. They all fell.

During the ensuing meeting he felt prompted by God to 'call all those who want a blessing. I walked over to the first person and said, "In the name of Je. . ." I did not even have time to say "sus" when the power of God threw that person to the floor.'

This pattern was repeated and several spoke in tongues or were unable to move. An anxious Howard-Browne turned to the local pastor: 'It wasn't me! It wasn't me!'

The 'anointing' remained strong for another two weeks and then subsided. A desire for consistent power for ministry was born.

As the years unfolded Rodney married Adonica and they had three children. He helped pioneer a church and was for two years an associate of Ray McCauley at the Johannesburg Rhema Church; a huge Word of Faith church associated with the work of Kenneth Hagin.

Rodney felt called however to America. He moved his family to Orlando, Florida, in 1987 and, virtually penniless, began slowly to build an itinerant preaching ministry. He had a quiet two years, and then in 1989 had another land-mark experience similar to the one in the Methodist church ten years before. He describes what happened in *Touch of God*:

It started taking place in April of 1989. I had to make adjustments in my ministry. I didn't ask God that these things would begin to happen. I just said, 'Lord, I am so hungry to see Your power displayed to touch people's lives. Please move. Do whatever You want to do.'

We were in a series of meetings in Albany, New York. It was the time we began to have two meetings per day. Both my wife and I were hungry for God to move. We had such a desire to see the glory of the Lord made manifest.

I remember the Tuesday morning meeting. As I was preaching, the glory of the Lord came into the building. I felt it just like someone put a heavy blanket upon me and the presence of the Lord filled the house.

A lady was sitting about three rows back and I noticed she was blinking and looking at the ceiling. I stopped what I was doing and said, 'Lady, what is wrong?' She told me nothing was wrong.

Then she said that as she was sitting there, she saw a thick fog or mist, like a cloud, come down and fill the room. The lights and the ceiling disappeared. It reminded her of growing up in a coastal town where in the early hours of the morning the mist was so thick you could only see a few feet in front of you.

I did not see this cloud, but I felt it. At that time, I called two people from the sound booth and they came walking down the aisle. When they got two-thirds of the way down the aisle, they fell under the power of God. No one touched them. Later they informed me that as they were walking down the aisle, they walked into a thick fog or mist and fell under the power with not even a hand being laid upon them.

While I was preaching, the power of God began to fall. Many people began to fall out of their seats. It looked like someone was shooting them and in some places whole rows at a time would go down. They were laughing and crying and falling all over the place and looked like drunken people.

I tried to preach above the noise of the people but to no avail. The glory of the Lord fell in such a wonderful way. Some were healed in their seats. The Lord then said to me, 'I will move all the time if you will allow me to.'

Howard-Browne was increasingly seeing the miraculous in

his meetings. While ministering in an Hispanic church in Chicago he spoke in other tongues. He didn't know a word of Spanish but someone ran up to him and said, 'You're speaking perfect Spanish!' He had been inviting the people to 'come to the paradise'.

The fledgling evangelist was still running a relatively small ministry. He had taken a correspondence course with the Pentecostal-oriented School of Bible Theology in San Jacinto, California and earned a doctorate of ministry.

He operated on a day-to-day basis, working on the principle that he would go and preach where he believed the pastor or church leadership was hungry for revival. He paid his own expenses and accepted love offerings.

Waiting to appear on a television broadcast he told staff that he would go to minister in the first place that someone called from. To his consternation someone called from Nome, in Alaska. The icy town of about 30,000 was an uninviting prospect but the tone was set on the first night when a lady got up out of her wheelchair after eighteen years of being crippled by arthritis. Rodney wasn't particularly praying for her to be healed. She had slumped 'under the power' and was trembling and shaking.

'What do you want to do?' he asked.

'Get up,' she said. He prayed, and she testified to a fire going through her. She got up and walked. 'The place came unglued'. It was the talk of the town.

Thirty-six churches were eventually represented at the meetings, with 3,000 people – 10% of the population – attending at some point during the ensuing weeks. The lady was a common sight on local streets where people would literally come up to her and exclaim over her healing.

The chain of events that would lead to the momentous spring of 1993 had begun.

The Nome pastor sent him to Fargo, North Dakota. He ministered in a jail there and accepted an invitation to minister at the church of the chaplain's brother. Howard-Browne

flew to this church after a South African crusade that saw
3,800 in attendance on the final evening. It was not an auspicious success: 'There was no response, no hallelujahs, no
amens. They were Pentecostals but they had lost Pentecost
years ago.'

Among the crowd there was a pastor. He handed Rodney
his card and invited him to his church. Much to the pastor's
surprise Rodney said he would be with him three days later.
This mission was better and a tent had to be erected to cope
with the crowds. The pastor sent him to his brother in a
church near west Palm Beach. Rodney returned to Florida, a
place with mixed memories for him. Some years before he
had walked weeping through Disneyworld: 'Thousands
come to see a mouse. Lord, when are they going to come to
see you?'

The crusade was excellent and a 1,000-seater tent had to
be erected. A man with several broken ribs, a history of
epilepsy after an assault, a damaged arm and more was
healed after falling down under the power. Howard-Browne
was taken aback as the newly healed man waved his arms
and punched himself in the ribs in amazement at the healing
that had taken place.

News of these meetings reached Karl Strader of the Carpenter's Home Church, an Assemblies of God church in
Lakeland, Florida. An astonished Rodney heard him speak
of them on television and of his own hunger for revival.

This was Rodney's kind of pastor and soon he had committed to a crusade at the 1,900-member church. The church
building could seat 10,000, but they had been through a split.
Karl Strader was therefore desperate for God to move and
gave Howard-Browne free reign. Strader used his media
influence to put Howard-Browne on Christian television and
to broadcast the meetings on a huge local radio station.

The meetings started small at 1,500, but by the fourth
week crowds of over 8,000 were filling the building. Rodney
was ill, but continued to minister. 'I'd been waiting for years

for this move of God and now physically I felt like I was dying. I said to God, "Lord, I know I'm nothing, but if you can use me I'll be happy."'

For Rodney what was happening felt like revival – Christians were being returned to their first love and an average of 1,000 people a week were giving their lives to Christ. They eventually baptised 2,260 people, sometimes not finishing the meetings until 2 am as a result. Over 500 churches were represented during the eight weeks of meetings at Carpenter's Home Church in 1993. The radio broadcasts over central Florida had helped attract an estimated 100,000 different people to the meetings.

Rodney, remembering his tears in Disneyworld, wept again one night. 'They're coming to get a touch from you Lord, not to see a mouse.'

Karl Strader, with 800 new members at his church, was a happy man. He told *Charisma* magazine, 'It was like something from the history books. People were flying in from Africa, Great Britain and Argentina to see it. . . I'd never seen anything like it.'

The meetings had been characterised by liberal doses of 'holy joy'. Joyce Strader, Karl's wife, told the readers of *Ministries Today* of the impact of laughter on one man:

Another man tells of his own change, as well as the change in his boss: 'For the last seven years I've worked the 11 pm to 7 am shift in a convenience store. The pay isn't much, the work is boring, stressful, frustrating – sometimes downright dangerous. My attitude was 100 percent bad.

'My boss and I were much the same. She lived to pass judgement on anyone unlucky enough to cross her the wrong way. Sales reps dreaded coming to our store, which they called "the convenience store from hell."

'But one sales rep was persistent about inviting the boss to the revival at our church. She refused at first but came the next night.

'Several nights later she and two others came into the store late, laughing hysterically. They had just come from the church. They invited one employee to go to another meeting the next night, but he told them, "I'm not into that." However, two days later he went and gave his heart to Jesus.

'I've watched God take a cold-hearted, spiteful woman and anoint her by his Spirit. It's now a blessing to work with her,' he said.

The impact of Rodney's ministry was not limited to the short term. Many leaders saw sustained renewal in their churches after attending his revival meetings.

Charisma, reflecting on the Boston-based Christian Teaching and Worship Center (CTWC), commented: 'All those who experienced this new bolt of the Holy Spirit's power at CTWC, including the leaders Paul and Mona Johnian, said they were initially sceptical of the spontaneous, boisterous laughter that interrupted their worship services in the autumn of 1993.'

Mona Johnian was struggling to come to terms with the laughing phenomena at a Rodney Howard-Browne meeting in Georgia when her own pastor, Bill Ligon, went forward for prayer. 'Bill is the epitome of dignity, a man totally under control.' When the evangelist prayed for him, Ligon 'fell on the stage' as if overcome. Mona Johnian's doubts began to recede.

Charisma magazine comments: 'The manifestation of holy laughter, the Johnians maintain, is more than an emotional outburst or a charismatic fad. It has been accompanied by forgiveness, emotional healing, a desire to witness, and healing of relationships.'

The blessing was also crossing over into the mainline denominations.

Hugh Williams of Christ the King, an Anglican church in Lakeland, Florida, told his parishioners:

Under the ministry of South African evangelist Rodney Howard-Browne, God changed my life, my family, my ministry, and my parish.

While attending my third revival meeting I was singled out for prayer as Brother Rodney moved about the congregation. I fell to the ground and broke into robust laughter for twenty minutes. This resulted in deliverance for some hurt feelings, a mild depression, and two years of restlessness which caused me to look for a new church. On another occasion God cleansed my heart from a persistent impurity. The result is most evident in my renewed marriage. Even my children notice the difference. I have not been the same since.

Revival hit the parish on Palm Sunday and has grown in intensity ever since. Dozens have come to Jesus or have been renewed in their relationship with Him. Attendance is up 40% over last year (112% on the Day of Pentecost). The budget is in the black for the first time in two years, and we have collected record-breaking offerings for ministries outside the church. A vestry meeting which closed with prayer resulted in the Treasurer and Junior Warden on the floor of the church because they were unable to get up. (I locked the door, called their wives, and told them their husbands were down at the church drunk. . . drunk in the Holy Ghost.)

One thing is for sure. I deserved none of this. But that is what 'grace' is – the undeserved, unmerited favour of God. It was God who first began to move. All I did was to say, 'Yes, God, I am hungry. Move in me.'

Rodney was apparently bemused himself on one occasion, as people laughed even while he spoke on hell. He reflected that hundreds came forward to be saved, nevertheless. He was invited to speak at Oral Roberts University and Rhema Bible College in Tulsa and witnessed astonishing scenes as over 4, 000 waited in line on one occasion to receive prayer.

He was winning many friends. Julia Dunn, writing in *Charisma* commented, 'His appeal is evident. It lies in his utter lack of slick evangelism. His simple style and genuine desire to unleash spiritual revival in America have caught the attention of charismatics who are eager to see signs and wonders.'

Influential charismatic publisher Steven Strang counselled care in a column in *Charisma* lest the laughter take over, but said: 'In the past year I have come to know Rodney personally. I believe he is humble, teachable and sincere. He seems intent on giving the glory to God. I urge Rodney Howard-Browne and others who are seeing similar manifestations to be careful, to test the spirits and to submit to godly counsel in order to keep this new revival balanced. On the other hand, we need to be aware that significant changes seem to be taking place in people's lives when the joy of the Lord touches them.'

Rodney prayed for a Vineyard pastor named Randy Clark at a meeting in Tulsa. Clark led a series of meetings subsequently at the Airport Vineyard in Toronto. The impact rocketed around the world. In the spring and early summer of 1994 Rodney also prayed for influential British church leaders Bryn Jones and Terry Virgo. The 'times of refreshing' in Britain began to gather pace as a result of the impact of these men and the influence of the Toronto Airport Vineyard.

The anointing

Any understanding of Rodney Howard-Browne's ministry will need to look at his theology of the 'anointing'. A close examination of his book *The Touch of God* reveals his perspective.

> The anointing is not some mystical something out there. The anointing is the presence and power of God manifested. We could say that the anointing is the manifest presence of God.
>
> There is a vast difference between the omnipresence of God and the manifest presence of God. The Lord is omnipresent but He is not manifesting or displaying His power everywhere. When God's power does manifest, something is going to happen. We read in Luke 5:17 that the power of the Lord was present to heal. When God walks in something happens, something takes place. The anointing is tangible. It can be felt. Just as electricity is tangible, so the anointing is tangible.

This does not mean that Browne perceives God's 'presence' to be an impersonal force. He writes 'The Holy Spirit. . . [is] a person.' He has published a booklet making more explicit the personhood of the Holy Spirit.

Elsewhere he uses the familiar image of the wind to describe how this 'manifest presence' or 'anointing' is apprehended. 'You can't see the wind, but you can see the results when it blows.'

Jesus, we are told in Acts 10:38, was anointed with the Holy Ghost and power. God was with him and healing and deliverance resulted. 'Every believer is anointed when they get born again. God comes and makes His home on the inside of us.'

Rodney believes however that those who are called to the five-fold ministries of Ephesians 4 – pastor, teacher, evangelist, apostle and prophet – and who are set apart for those tasks, will have 'a greater manifestation of the nine gifts of the Spirit, and a greater anointing than the laity'.

He uses the analogy of a well and a river to further explain how the Holy Spirit's anointing is made tangible.

> In John 4:13 Jesus said, 'Whosoever drinketh of the water that I shall give him shall never thirst; but the water that I shall give him shall be in him a well of water springing up into everlasting life.' I want you to notice it says a well. The scripture says, 'With joy shall ye draw water out of the wells of salvation' (Isaiah 12:3). We could call this first anointing a 'well' anointing.
>
> 'In the last day, that great day of the feast, Jesus stood and cried, saying, "If any man thirst let him come unto me, and drink. He that believeth on me, as the scripture hath said, out of his belly shall flow rivers of living water." (But this spake he of the Spirit, which they that believe on him should receive: for the Holy Ghost was not yet given; because that Jesus was not yet glorified)' (John 7:37).
>
> In this scripture, we not only see a well, but something that is bigger than a well. We see a river. In other words, you can have a 'well' anointing when you get born again, and you can have a

'river' anointing when you get the baptism in the Holy Ghost.

Jesus told the disciples to tarry in Jerusalem for the coming of the Holy Spirit. He said in Acts 1:8, 'But ye shall receive power, after that the Holy Ghost is come upon you and ye shall be witnesses.'

An increase in the tangible presence of God or anointing on our lives flows from our relationship with him. 'Prayer must be used primarily to fellowship with the Lord and to spend time being filled up in His presence then out of an overflow of his touch, we minister to the needs of hurting humanity.'

Rodney calls people to immerse themselves in the life of Jesus:

> I believe another way to increase the anointing is to spend much time reading the gospels and following closely the ministry of Jesus. Jesus said, 'The Son can do nothing of himself, but what he seeth the Father do' (Jn 5:19). I believe we will only do what we see Jesus do.
>
> The disciples followed Jesus and saw the signs and wonders and miracles that He did. He said to them, 'He that believeth on me, the works that I do shall he do also; and greater works than these shall he do: because I go unto my Father' (Jn 14:12).
>
> He sent the Holy Ghost to empower them that they might go forth and do His works. Later, when Peter and John were taken in front of the chief priests and elders and commanded not to preach or teach in the name of Jesus, they said, 'We cannot but speak the things which we have seen and heard' (Acts 4:20).

The reason that many do not receive more power from God is because 'their thought-life is far from Him'. Those who desire an increase of the 'anointing' must be hungry for God to move and have a steadfast character.

> You must want the Holy Ghost. You must thirst for Him. You must desire the anointing more than anything else in life. You must want it more than you want life itself. You have to mean business with God, get serious with God. It is not a quick stroll down the aisle to have a hand slapped on your head. You have

to desire it, intensely desire it from the bottom of your heart and from the depths of your being. You cry out to God, 'Do whatever you have to do, but please, let me be a part of it. Do a work in my heart!' God can do a work in your heart.

Everyone wants a ministry, but no one wants to pay the price to become the vessel God wants. When we become hungry enough to do whatever it takes, God will fill us with fresh oil.

If we are going to be anointed, the one thing we have to do is repent. Repent. One thing that a child of God should be able to do more than anything is repent.

It is not a one-time experience either. 'I'm convinced in my heart this is a constant process for every child of God. We should daily be filled with the Holy Ghost. We should daily let the Spirit of God come on us. We should daily taste of the good things of the Lord.'

Because Rodney believes that the anointing is the tangible presence of God he also believes that the presence can be localised and that when someone asks God to work on their behalf, their placing of a demand on the anointing causes it to flow into them.

Speaking of the woman with the issue of blood (Mk 5:28-29) he comments:

In a crowd such as this, Jesus must have been bumped or touched by the multitudes. Yet something happened when this woman touched the hem of His garment. Divine virtue or power, called 'dunamis' in the Greek, flowed out of Jesus into her body and she was healed.

There are many other references to people touching Jesus and being healed. In the book of Acts, when the shadows of the apostles passed over the sick, they were healed.

Jesus spat on people. He also breathed on them and said 'Receive ye the Holy Ghost' (Jn 20:22). It's all a point of contact in which someone can release their faith.

There are many examples of this in the Bible from anointing oil in James 5:14, to anointed handkerchiefs and aprons in Acts 19:11, 12.

He believes therefore that the anointing is 'transferable'. He is wary of placing hands on someone hastily. 'It is not just symbolic – there is an actual transfer of the anointing.'

He quotes 1 Timothy 4:14: '"Do not neglect your gift, which was given you through a prophetic message when the body of elders laid their hands on you." When you take your hands, by the Spirit of God, and put them on somebody's head, the life of God on the inside of you flows out of you into them.'

Rodney is therefore careful about who prays for whom at his meetings. As a travelling evangelist and coping with huge crowds, the logistics of a 'ministry team' seem too much.

His Carpenter's Home meetings were infiltrated by a witch who prayed for people, so he keeps a close guard now and usually only he prays for people.

He is clear however that revival will not spring from the ministry of a mighty man. 'There will be no great men in the coming revival. There will be no great women in the coming revival. There will be ordinary men and ordinary women with a great God. They will rise up and tell the story of the cross.'

With this in mind he often calls out all the pastors in a meeting and prays that the Lord will impart a fresh anointing to them. *Charisma* reports on the revival that results.

Dale Stoll, a Mennonite pastor, says he had a powerful encounter with the Lord during a recent series of revival services. The revival took off following a February meeting with local pastors, most from conservative denominations. The services were conducted by a Vineyard pastor Tom McMillan of Fort Wayne who had been in meetings with Howard-Browne. 'It was an amazing encounter,' said Stoll. 'Almost immediately there were twenty-five pastors on the floor.'

The Howard-Browne enigma

Some of those hostile to the current renewal have seized on Rodney's roots in the Word of Faith movement, particularly his time as a pastor at Ray McCauley's Rhema Church in Johannesburg.

The Word of Faith movement is by no means a cohesive group, but within its camp the two most high-profile teachers are Kenneth Hagin and Kenneth Copeland. Their teaching emphasis has drawn considerable criticism from within the Pentecostal/charismatic movement. Oral Roberts University professor Charles Farah wrote of the presumptuous nature of some of what was taught in respect of health and wealth (*From the Pinnacle of the Temple*). Dan McConnell sought to demonstrate similarities between their teaching and Christian Science style groups (*A Different Gospel*). Hank Hanegraaf, writing in the best-selling *Christianity in Crisis* examined their theology of Christians as 'little gods' and the belief that Jesus died 'spiritually' in hell and literally became sinful.

There is not space here to begin to unpack the arguments. Suffice it to say that many feel that some word of faith teachings go beyond the boundaries of orthodoxy. I certainly do.

The argument therefore goes: Howard-Browne is from the faith camp; they're unorthodox; this 'time of refreshing' is therefore a deception.

It isn't quite as simple as that, however, for several reasons. The first is in Rodney's general independence of mind. He gives short shrift in his books to several controversial charismatic doctrines or areas of debate:

On heavy shepherding: 'God does not give ministers the right to usurp his authority or brutalise the sheep.'

On tongues fanaticism: 'Some people think He said, "You will receive tongues." What good are tongues without the power? We have many babbling believers with very little power.'

On extreme spiritual warfare: Rodney describes some spiritual warfare theology as a 'Honey, I Blew up the Devil' distraction. 'The greatest soul winners have never indulged in such practices.' He counsels doing the works of Jesus and warns against 'doctrine derived from novels'.

On prophecy: Rodney maintains that this should be 'confirmation' not 'information'. He warns that persistent 'inaccurate prophecy' causes disillusioned people to miss out on the real prophetic word.

On accountability: Rodney warns against leaders who 'have no relationships with anyone' and are surrounded by 'yes' people. He warns that once they're on a fund-raising treadmill the crisis letters become inevitable.

Another indication of his independence of mind is his acknowledged debt to nineteenth-century revivalist Charles Finney, who like Rodney rose to prominence in his late twenties, and also saw scenes of great emotion in his meetings. He is also an admirer of the Pentecostal healing evangelist and 'man of great faith', Smith Wigglesworth.

Rodney is unafraid to hold his own independent opinions and neither wants to be, nor can easily be, pigeonholed.

He will not be drawn into criticism of Hagin and Copeland. 'They're people of integrity. You couldn't leave their presence without knowing that you've been with someone who loves Jesus with all their heart. Could I get up and say I don't agree with these men, they're not of God? No, not at all. I know them. I've watched their lives.'

This is tempered with the qualifying statement, 'Would I like to be polarised, locked into that camp? No, not at all. I'm not part of a camp.'

Those willing to comb through Rodney's books will find familiar Word-of-Faith style comments. 'I believe in prosperity,' he asserts. '. . .Whenever the word of God is spoken in faith from the lips of a believer then God's healing power is activated . . . Paul's thorn in the flesh was not an illness.'

But there are also vigorous critiques of the excesses of

faith ministry and indications of a more moderate Pente-costal orthodoxy. 'This last day revival will not come through a single group or denomination. Rather, it will come through a blood-washed church. . .'

The mention of the blood of Christ is instructive given the belief among some Word-of-Faith teachers that the blood of Christ did not atone for our sins.

Some faith teachers also believe our words can be cre-ative and that this is because of 'laws', which means God must honour. Rodney is quite clear that the power is all God's. 'The Lord then said to me, "You are just a vessel through which I am flowing. You cannot earn this anointing; it's given as I will. If I gave you a key and you could get this anointing at anytime, you would begin to think it's all you and not Me. Because you know it is Me that is doing this, you will have to give Me all the glory."'

Referring to the lady who got out of the wheelchair in Nome, Rodney commented on his view of healing: 'If God wants to come down and heal, let him come down and heal. It's God's business.'

This stance, broadly similar to the Vineyard position, is some way away from the militant 'claim your healing' ethos of some faith teachers.

In his booklet *The Coming Revival* he is also frank in his wariness of faith teaching excesses:

'I'm in the Word! Did you make your confessions today? A confession a day will keep the devil away!'

You try to talk to people. Maybe you ask a simple question: 'How are you doing today?'

'I'm blessed. Praise God, hallelujah, I'm the righteousness of God in Christ Jesus. Hallelujah, I cannot be defeated, and I will not quit. Hallelujah, I'm the head and not the tail!'

'Brother, how are you?'

'I'm blessed, brother. Praise God.'

But when you looked out of the window, his car was being towed away!

If a man came in on crutches and you asked, 'How are you?' he would say, 'I'm healed and whole. Hallelujah, I don't have a problem.'

In some instances, you could never relate to some people!

Then the excesses came. Everyone had to have a Brand X watch and drive an XYZ car, or they didn't have the anointing. And everyone had to get in agreement with you. 'Would you get in agreement with me, brother? Please be in agreement with me.'

I've gone to some churches in the States where the speaker has got up and said, 'Today I want to talk about twenty ways to become prosperous and get a new car.'

I think, 'God, have mercy! We're through with all that junk. Who cares what kind of car you drive? God doesn't care what car you drive.'

His overall stance can perhaps be best understood in his conception of unity.

I will be honest with you. There are ministers whom I don't personally agree with. But I will tell you I know beyond a shadow of a doubt that the hand of the Lord is upon their lives. I rejoice that many lives are being touched by the power of God through their ministries. You have to be spiritually closed not to see that God is using them, even if you don't agree one hundred percent with their teachings or the way they look at things. If we can agree to disagree, we can all climb the mountain together.

There is no simple explanation of the Howard-Browne enigma. Suffice it to say that a simplistic dismissal of him as a Word-of-Faith extremist is not adequate given the overview of his thinking presented above.

7

The Finger of God

When renewal and revival come, as they appear to have done in 1994, how can the Christian judge what is of God and what is superficial? Jonathan Edwards, a leader in an eighteenth-century revival, has wisdom for those seeking the fingerprints of God.

Jonathan Edwards was a significant figure in the revival which swept New England between 1740 and 1742. A Reformed minister, whose books are published by the conservative Banner of Truth publishing house, Edwards was no emotional enthusiast. His writings have become regarded as classics. His book *Distinguishing Marks of a Work of the Spirit of God* (Banner of Truth) is full of wisdom for those seeking to understand the current wave of refreshing and renewal.

Jonathan Edwards establishes his ground rules straight away as he encourages his readers to avoid 'over-credulousness' and to 'test the spirits' (1 Jn 4:1), so as to avoid being taken in by false prophets. He is clear that we are to 'take the Scriptures as our guide'.

He then looks at common objections to revival, suggests positive fruit and encourages careful leadership by the church leaders of the day.

Let us look first at his response to objections to revival.

The unusual and the extraordinary

'What the church has been used to is not a rule by which we are to judge,' warns Edwards. Within Scripture rules he observes: 'We ought not to limit God where he has not limited himself.' Noting that people's minds may be greatly influenced and moved to strong emotions of fear, sorrow, desire, love and joy but that change may also come quietly, he counsels his readers not to fall into the trap of those who scoffed at the new and unusual nature of Pentecost (Acts 2:13; 26:24).

Should we not expect Pentecost-type scenes, he conjectures, during that 'last and greatest outpouring of the Spirit of God that is to be in the latter ages of the world'?

Objections to physical effects

He records that some have been overtaken by 'tears, trembling, groans, loud outcries, agonies of body, or the failing of bodily strength'. Edwards argues that this is not conclusive proof that God is at work, but it may well be because of 'the influence of the Spirit of God'. He argues that Scripture does not 'expressly or indirectly exclude such effects on the body, nor does reason exclude them'.

He seems to suggest that if the mind is impressed with 'the misery of hell' or other aspects of the greatness and awesomeness of God, it is little wonder that a person should tremble. He cites times of war or danger as the source of great emotion and is not surprised that the convicted sinner should feel strongly too.

To those who argue that there is no New Testament precedent, he responds: 'Nobody supposes that there is any need of express Scripture for every external, accidental manifestation of the inward motion of the mind.' What are we to say, he asks, about the falling and trembling of the Philippian jailer as he came under conviction? Did not the disciples cry out in fear during the storm (Mt 14:26)?

Edwards is a little impatient with those who object on these grounds. He describes them as frivolous, and wonders by what rule the objectors will judge anything positively. He counsels looking at the 'root and cause' of things and seeking to discern the fruit in a person's life.

Unhelpful publicity

Some appeared to be fretting that revival was 'causing a notable, visible and open commotion'. What about the opposition to the early church in Jerusalem or Samaria, Antioch, Ephesus and Corinth?

Dreams and visions

Those touched by the Spirit were having vivid dreams and visions. Edwards is cautious about how these are interpreted but he rebuffs vigorously those who would despise them. 'I dare appeal to any man of the greatest powers of mind, whether he is able to fix his thoughts on God, or Christ, or the things of another world, without imaginary ideas attending his meditations.' It is no argument that the Spirit is not at work, he counters, simply because some were caught up in a 'kind of ecstasy'. He neither places these dreams and visions on a par with the biblical prophets, nor brings in 'the help of the devil into the account we give to these things'.

The emotion of crowds

Edwards had no problem with the idea that some are influenced by the effect of the Spirit on others.

Arguing that actions sometimes speak louder than words, he concludes that 'it is therefore no argument against the goodness of the effect that persons are greatly affected seeing others so'.

He notes that any means of spreading the gospel produces its 'stony ground' hearers, but is adamant that even the most intellectual of men and women make decisions that are not rooted in rational, linear logic, and that being moved by the unspoken message in the sorrow or joy of others is not wrong, if reinforced by the word of God being proclaimed.

Edwards seems to anticipate that God works both through sovereign acts and the testimony and example of believers, and cites Zechariah 8:21-23: 'And the inhabitants of one city shall go to another, saying, "Let us go speedily to pray before the Lord."'

'But, Lord, some of these people are so extreme!'

As I read Edwards for this chapter, I wondered whether his wit was deliberate or whether I was just reading humour into his remarks. One of the best one-liners of his book runs as follows: 'We are to consider that the end for which God pours out his Spirit is to make men holy and not to make them politicians.' Noting that some who seem to be touched by the Spirit are 'imprudent and irregular' he reflects: 'It is no wonder that in a mixed multitude of all souls – wise and unwise, young and old, of weak and strong abilities, under strong impressions of mind – there are many who behave themselves imprudently.'

He is adamant that 'a thousand imprudences will not prove a work to be not of the Spirit of God'. Given the weakness of human nature and the residue of sin in even the most zealous believer, it is not unusual for there to be some unhelpful behaviour. 'What about the church of Corinth?' he rumbles, warming to the subject, 'or the Apostle Peter, who had to be confronted by Paul over his wavering about eating with the non-Jewish believers?' (Gal 2:11-13).

Errors of judgement and delusions of Satan

Without the recent memory of the words of the Lord that the disciples had, we are bound to be fallible, he argues. Nor should we be surprised if there are 'false miracles at the same time, by the hand of the devil'. True miracles occurred in Bible times even though there were false healers. He further argues that some may be godly and yet in some things be deluded. He particularly refers to the issue of prophecy. Many responsible charismatics today would share his contention, even while hanging on to the weighed prophecy baby as they empty out the superficial prophecy bathwater.

Gross errors and scandals

Edwards' militant pursuit of balance is maintained, even in the face of the worst excesses. He warns against guilt by association. A study of church history will reveal, he suggests, that there is 'no instance of any great revival of religion' which has not 'witnessed gross heresies'. Hebrews 6 implies that those who have known the Spirit may still fall into error. Judas, one of Jesus' inner circle, proved to be a morally bankrupt man. Nicholas, one of the Jerusalem church deacons, is held by some to be head of the Nicolatian sect so roundly condemned in Revelation 2:6.

Hellfire and brimstone

Were the preachers of the day frightening their listeners into the kingdom? Edwards calmly counters: 'If I am in danger of going to hell, I should be glad to know as much as I possibly can of the dreadfulness of it.' With lives and eternal destinies at stake, passionate preaching is to be expected.

Responding to criticism that people are frightened along the path to heaven's door, he reflects: 'I think it is a reasonable thing to frighten persons away from hell.'

The fruits of revival

Having carefully responded to the critics of revival, Edwards warms to the core of his presentation. What are the positive fruits, reflected in Scripture, of a genuine move of God? He outlines five:

1. Jesus is honoured

When the Holy Spirit comes, the person of Jesus is esteemed by all those genuinely touched. Edwards believes that this will spill out from intellectual assent into testimony, declaration and confession that 'Christ is Lord'.

It's the Spirit, he argues, if the hearers are moved to 'belief in the history of Christ as he appeared in the flesh – and that he is the son of God and was sent of God to save sinners, that he is the only Saviour and that they stand in great need of him'. The devil does not promote counterfeit revival with this type of fruit. Edwards thunders: 'He mortally hates the story and doctrine of [Christ's] redemption.' It is not the devil's intention to see Christ glorified and his wisdom followed (1 Cor 12:3).

2. A detachment from selfish pleasure or gain

Edwards, quoting 1 Corinthians 2:15-16, argues that the 'world', which the believer no longer loves, refers to the corruptions and lusts of men, and the 'acts and objects by which they are gratified'. The Spirit is at work, he suggests, if there is a reduction in men's desire for the 'pleasure, profits and honours of the world'.

Only the irrational, he adamantly suggests, would say that the devil makes people more 'careful, inquisitive and watchful to discern what is sinful, and to avoid future sins; and so be more afraid of the devil's temptations, and be more careful to guard against them'.

You may not like the shrieking, fainting or crying, he implies, but if the lifestyle is changed, then it is the Holy

Spirit who is at work. Satan would not cast out Satan (Mt 12:25-26).

3. A hunger for the Scriptures

Another pithy Edwards sentence wraps the truth up in a way we can grasp. 'A spirit of delusion will not incline persons to seek direction at the mouth of God. . . Every text is a dart to torment the old serpent'.

4. Dwelling on truth

The Holy Spirit at work in revival draws men and women to the truth, not error. If people become aware of their rebellion against God and their own helplessness and are agreeable to sound doctrine, we should be thanking God. Look at the fruits, he contends. Be more open and not so cautious.

5. Loving one another

When the Spirit of God is at work, he 'quells contentions among men, gives a spirit of peace and goodwill, excites to acts of outward kindness and earnest desires for the salvation of souls, and causes a delight in those that appear as the children of God and followers of Christ'.

This love can be counterfeited by the selfish and deceived, but true Christian love is marked by humility and patience (1 Cor 12:4-5).

Humility and love are aspects of the character of God and run counter to the marks of the devil, malice and pride.

Edwards' argument climaxes as he urges his readers to observe the fruit of changed lives, rather than question 'whatever means a sovereign God. . . employs to carry it on'. The fruit of a changed lifestyle outweighs 'a thousand such little objections' based on oddities, irregularities, delusions and scandals.

'The devil,' he argues, 'may seek to mimic visions, revelations, prophecies and miracles', but he cannot drive people to the truth, exalt Jesus, or bring about real ethical change in people's lives.

Warnings and encouragement

Edwards now prepares himself for the final lap. He has run the gauntlet of objections and established the positive fruits of renewal. Now he must continue in the race, armed with practical wisdom and wary of pitfalls.

He has admitted earlier that revival is contagious in some instances. He also points out that it can break out spontaneously. He contends that as time goes by the fruit of change will emerge and he speaks of people well known to him and whom he has observed over several months.

He further observes that many who were overtaken with tears, trembling or prostration remained 'in perfect exercise of their reason' and subsequently 'were well able to give an account of the circumstances of their mind'.

He identifies his own broad sympathies with those who would moan about the disruption of the usual order of things. He is not about to be legalistic however. If it happens, it happens. 'I do not think this is confusion or an unhappy interruption, any more than if a company should meet on the field to pray for rain and should be broken off from their exercise by a plentiful shower.' The genuineness of any spiritual change, he warns, is not related to its physical impact, but its long-term effect on the life of the believer.

He has some practical warnings and encouragements:

1. The need for wise leadership

'A people in such circumstances stand in great and continued need of guides, and their guides stand in continued need of much more wisdom than they have of their own.'

2. Caution before criticism

He sounds a solemn warning: 'Let us all be hence warned, by no means to oppose or do anything in the least to clog or hinder the work; but, on the contrary, do our utmost to promote it.'

He warns those who would call it a work of the devil to beware that they do not sin against the Holy Ghost. He promotes a 'principle of prudence' that is neither over-enthusiastic nor merely spectating.

He wryly observes: 'If they want to see a work of God without difficulties or stumbling blocks, it will be like the fools waiting at the riverside to have the water all run by.'

Don't be like those who prayed for Christ's coming, he warns, and then would neither acknowledge nor receive him.

Don't rely on the second-hand criticisms of others, Edwards counsels. He refers to the lesson of Gamaliel who said that if the apostles' work was not of God, it would come to nought. If it was, their opponents would be fighting God.

Get off the fence, Edwards implores his fellow ministers, as he prods them to get involved, suggesting that silence is a kind of secret opposition. 'He that is not with us is against us.' Don't provoke God, he admonishes.

3. Stay humble

Be careful of spiritual pride. Beware of believing that the 'secret of the Lord is especially with us' or that we are 'extraordinary ambassadors of heaven'.

Edwards then shares his thoughts on the extraordinary gifts of the Spirit and his belief that love is far more important than these. He does not desire a restoration of these gifts. Many of those who currently quote him, myself included, will want to differ with him on this point, while heeding his warnings about excess. Further chapters of this book will particularly examine the pastoral response to a growth of prophecy.

4. Don't despise the mind

With the Spirit moving powerfully, some are inclined to neglect human learning and study. God made use of Paul's learning as well as the wisdom of Solomon and Moses.

Edwards does not deny the likelihood of spontaneous speech and Spirit-inspired words. He warmly encourages a backbone of method, however, particularly in sermon preparation, so that people can both understand and memorise the word.

5. Censure of others

Edwards is not averse to believers challenging others about doctrine, as his earlier reference to the disputes between Paul and Peter shows.

He waxes lyrical, however, about those who make more fundamental judgements about other Christians, and denounces them as wicked, hypocritical or ignorant of 'real religion'. 'Only God can know the hearts of men' (1 Kings 8:39; Rom 14:4). Given our own pride, prejudice and partiality, we should be careful not to condemn others.

He also cautions those who are friends of the revival to beware an 'angry zeal' when they are responding to critics. Be like Christ, he counsels, who remained quiet and dignified in the face of attacks, insults and trial. Be like Paul, who encouraged Timothy to be 'gentle unto all men. . . in meekness instructing those that oppose themselves'.

The formalism/freedom balance

Edwards warns against a rigid formalism, but seems wary of innovation for the sake of novelty. Don't despise tradition, he seems to say. Express the truth by the most appropriate means for the people to whom you are talking (1 Cor 9:20-23).

We can learn much by listening to the voice of church history and the wisdom of those who have faced similar situations to ours and have already searched the Scriptures.

With Edwards' words about wise response to censure at the forefront of my mind I have sought to carefully consider the mass of material already issued which seeks to criticise what is currently happening. Having had my own misgivings in the early days of this time of refreshing I can easily understand the genuine doubts that some may have. The biblical model of the Bereans who searched the Scripture to verify what they were hearing and seeing is a good one to follow.

There are however four characteristics which are the hallmark of some of the more militant writings and sermons that have criticised this current time of refreshing. Many of the issues they raise are dealt with elsewhere in this book. As you read critical documents you may like to question their analysis in the light of the following.

It is clear from Scripture that although the church is to be careful of judging men and women's hearts, there is a responsibility for us all to be careful and discerning. Paul reproved Peter for falling into legalistic attitudes against non-Jewish believers. The epistle of John encourages us to 'test the spirits'. We are told to discover what those we deal with believe about Christ.

At a time like this, when strange or unusual things are happening in national church life, it often seems that people abandon proper biblical discernment and display a latent intolerance and impatience. Because these issues are so serious to so many, an ungracious word or ill-thought-out opinion can undermine and destroy, rather than illuminate and correct. It seems that many are ready to speak out condemnatory judgement with little thought of the consequences.

Snap judgements

It is easy to dismiss something because we are wary of the key personnel involved. One pastor, contacted during my research, dismissed the possibility of revival or renewal when he learned who was involved. Many of us know people who have held extreme doctrines or behaved insensitively, but then grown into maturity and graciousness. Dismissing something on the basis of old history makes no allowance for change and progress.

Others attend one meeting, view it through their own grid of expectations, leave the meeting and denounce it vigorously. Did they really find out what had taken place in people's lives? Did they find out if the church was still on a 'learning curve' in terms of appropriate discernment and sensitive discipline?

Would we leave the Corinthian church, the wild men of their day, to their heretical devices, or like Paul, acknowledge their fervour and seek to bring gentle reproof?

Unresearched judgement

One current leaflet in circulation makes extensive allegations about the ministry of a particular group of churches. A cursory reading of this group's books, magazine and tapes would cause any reasonable person to query the accuracy of the allegations. Another leaflet in circulation brands someone as demonised on the basis of a newspaper report.

It is not surprising that the world considers us extremists and bigots if we give opinions that will help shape the attitudes of those who trust us without ensuring that our facts are correct and our information is complete.

Unrighteous judgement

We should always seek to give those on the receiving end of criticism a chance to respond. This process would usually happen in response to something that was written by the organisation or individual involved, and that had provoked controversy. This gives them the opportunity to put their remarks in context.

We should only go public when we are aware that a

vigorous 'behind the scenes' dialogue has already taken place and that no change in stance is apparent.

It's disturbing, however, when Christians simply dismiss one another on the basis of hearsay and selective reading. Any public denunciation, in church or in print, that does not observe the principle of Matthew 18:15-17 has to be questioned.

Have we met the local representatives of those we criticise? Were there witnesses? One famous critique of a particular movement, currently quoted by many, is based on a no-witnesses, off-the-record corridor conversation, which was printed without confirming with the person attacked that he had been quoted correctly.

Has the matter been raised with the local, national or international leadership of those we criticise? Only when we have sought dialogue and it has been rebuffed or broken down can we righteously air our public misgivings about named individuals or organisations in the body of Christ.

Legalistic and illogical judgements

Heresy hunters delight in playing the guilt-by-association game. Compare what is happening today to the activities of a group in history, and you may quickly be reminded of the current unorthodox attitudes of that group, and so be warned that you are on the slippery slope to heresy.

On that basis we would strike Wesley and J.C. Ryle off our list of reliable spiritual resources because sections of Methodism and Anglicanism have been captured by heretics and Scripture twisters.

The ghost of theological perfectionism haunts our dialogues. Most of us don't write Luther off completely because he was anti-Semitic, we don't dismiss Wesley, despite his imbalance on perfectionism.

We respect Calvin, despite the fact he used the state against his enemies. We respect General Booth, despite his elimination of baptism and communion from Salvation Army practice.

Sometimes we will want to challenge the belief systems of our fellow believers, and may, after dialogue, alert the wider church to our concerns. But don't we owe it to each other, as fellow Christians, and to the name of the Lord we worship, to be more careful about rushing to judgement? There's too much at stake for us to be fighting each other.

8

Shaken and Stirred

Media coverage of the so-called 'Toronto blessing' has often majored on the extreme physical reactions experienced by some. The phenomena of shaking, laughter, prostration and visionary experiences are by no means new in recent church history. They have been a feature of charismatic church life since the first stirrings of renewal in the early sixties, and gained greater prominence as the Vineyard movement began to impact the United Kingdom. But they have never been so intense or so widespread.

As spiritual excitement grew in June 1994, some were already anticipating that the phenomena of renewal would cause controversy.

Nick Cuthbert, known to many for his pioneering work with the Birmingham Jesus Centre, is now the pastor of the 400-strong Riverside Fellowship. He says:

> In the middle of a meeting recently where a number of things were happening, I felt that the Lord showed me a river going out to sea. The tight boundaries of the church were going to be changed for the wide open sea – the church going out to the world. But the mouth of the river is a dangerous and often turbulent place. I felt God was saying we are in for a time of turbulence in preparation for his greater movings.
>
> This time is particularly a test of leadership. If not handled right it will provoke disruption and division in the church. We

115

need to be refreshed and released, but we need to glue ourselves to the Scriptures and biblical understanding or there are going to be shipwrecks.

Remaining 'glued to the Scripture' is the instinctive reaction of most, but how should the Scriptures be interpreted?

Two key statements, both widely circulated, echo the views of Jonathan Edwards, who reminded his readers that the Scriptures didn't cater for every eventuality.

Gerald Coates, in a set of guideline notes sent to Pioneer leaders in August 1994 set out his perspective:

> There is plenty of biblical material covering all of these aspects, manifestations and reactions to the Spirit's presence. Some may regard biblical evidence for these manifestations as either slim or scarce. But it is well accepted, within biblical scholarship and evangelical circles, that the importance of an issue cannot be gauged based on the number of times it is mentioned in Scripture.
>
> For example, the phrase 'born again' is only mentioned two or three times in the entire New Testament; the breaking of bread is referred to on a handful of occasions; dancing, while referred to by our Lord in terms of how people responded to his ministry (Luke 7:32) is nevertheless not mentioned in the Epistles. But it is difficult to believe that in a culture where dancing on festive occasions was not only acceptable but promoted (see the Psalms!) that after the Messiah had come, forgiveness had been exercised, people groups had been reconciled and gifts of the Spirit had been poured out on people, they stopped dancing!
>
> Before we look at some of the manifestations of the Spirit, or people responding to the Spirit, it should also be noted the Bible was not given so that we could proof-text everything. Most evangelical Christians are currently engaged in a wide range of activities for which there are no proof texts.
>
> There are things God approves of in Scripture and we call them scriptural. But there are a lot of things that are plainly non-scriptural. The Bible is not a text book but a test book. We draw our experiences alongside Scripture to test whether they are of

God or not.

Things most Christians are involved in without much biblical data to support them include church buildings, communion/Lord's supper (where people do not eat a meal or even talk with one another), the gospel preached to the converted at 6.30 pm every Sunday evening, closing your eyes when you pray, sitting when you pray, saying 'grace' before meals, Sunday schools, youth clubs, women's meetings, and even a daily morning quiet time! That is not to say these things are wrong. The point is, God wants us to grow up, and between those things he specifically approves of and others he specifically disapproves of, we are given liberty to develop a wide range of activities.

The same liberty applies to manifestations of the Holy Spirit and reactions to the Holy Spirit (though it has been pointed out that even a manifestation is some kind of reaction to the presence and prompting of the Holy Spirit).

Bill Jackson of the Champaign Vineyard, Chicago, in an extensive document, *What in the World is Happening to Us?*, widely circulated via various Vineyard churches, also grasps the interpretation nettle.

When we ask, 'Is it biblical?', we're probably asking for what is commonly called a 'proof text'. A proof text is a portion of Scripture that, when taken in context, validates the particular position we are taking. In order to ascertain whether these phenomena are biblical, we need to lay down some ground rules for solid interpretation.

There are three basic doctrinal headings in the Bible:
1. Christian theology (what Christians are to believe)
2. Christian ethics (how Christians are to behave)
3. Christian experience or practice (what Christians are to do).

You can call a verse/passage a proof text when the writer clearly states what God wants us to believe, do or practise. These texts can be labelled 'primary'.

There are many beliefs, behaviours and practices, however, that are not clearly taught but rather are implied. These texts can be labelled 'secondary'. This doesn't mean unimportant, only that a clear statement cannot be found.

Let's take baptism for instance. The Bible clearly states that Christians are to be baptised. There is a primary text that says so in Matthew 28:19. *How* we are to be baptised, on the other hand, is never explicitly stated. This is why different groups baptise in different ways. There are, however, clear biblical passages that show that it was normal in the early church to immerse people in water. Even the word 'baptise' means to immerse. This doesn't prove that this is the way the church should baptise for all time. It does, however, imply it. At the very least it illustrates that this is what was done. The mode of baptism, therefore, is a secondary, not a primary issue.

When dealing with the supernatural phenomena, we are dealing with the area of Christian practice. There are no primary texts that clearly state that Christians are to fall down, shake or look drunk during seasons of divine visitation (although there are primary texts referring to prophetic revelation) but there are a number of secondary (remember, secondary does not mean invalid or unimportant) texts that illustrate that these were some of the responses people had during moments of divine visitation.

Later in this chapter an overview of the phenomena, with relevant scriptures, will be examined.

Wes Campbell, of the Canadian New Life Vineyard, in a document written in 1992, reflected on physical phenomena. 'More often than not the Bible tells us *what* to do but not *how*. It states *absolutes* but not *forms*. Hence in the sixteenth century many reformers destroyed the church organs because they were not "found in the Bible".'

Campbell urges us to adopt five criteria when examining the physical phenomena.

– Does it conform to the explicit or implicit word of God?
– Does it ultimately exalt the Lord Jesus Christ?
– Does it attack the kingdom of darkness?
– Does it produce spiritual fruit?

- What is the character of those involved in the practice?

As we progress through an examination of the phenomena, Campbell's essential thrust will emerge in the advice given or the apologetic offered by various leaders.

Evangelical leaders, not withstanding a Protestant wariness of appealing to church history or tradition, do look to historic precedent and the spiritual fruit of previous generations.

The 1859 revival in Ulster is perhaps a case in point. John Weir, writing in *Heaven Came Down* (Ambassador) might well have been speaking of Holy Trinity Brompton, not the parishes of Ballymena and Coleraine:

> From a carefully prepared report, drawn up by the writer of the foregoing and presented to the Synod of Ballymena and Coleraine, it appeared that 'in all directions prayer-meetings had sprung up, and that without number', and that 'the Spirit had descended in power'. Referring to the physical excitement, Mr Buick says, 'Through the instrumentality of the Word and prayer, convictions, often the most powerful, even to the *convulsing of the whole frame, the trembling of every joint, intense burning of heart, and complete prostration of strength*, have been produced. The arrow of conviction pierces the conscience, the heart swells nigh to bursting, a heavy and intolerable burden presses down the spirit, and the burdened, burning heart, unable to contain any longer, bursts forth in the piercing cry of distress, "Lord Jesus, have mercy on my sinful soul!" Under such convictions, the heart finds relief in pouring out its cries and tears before the Lord.
>
> Under the awakening of the dormant mind, the stirring up of the slumbering conscience, and the powerful movement of the nervous system, the imagination is often called into lively activity in picturing solemn scenes of the future, and in hearing words of warning and counsel. Such sights are easily accounted for, while they are often sanctified in producing saving impressions.'

It is worth noting that Weir mentions the role of prayer. As one who believes we need more and better preaching in this generation, I'm still wary of the revival-comes-only-through-preaching mindset. A careful reading of history would perhaps suggest that prayer, song, testimony, exhortation from unlearned new converts, and prayer all played their role in the public gatherings where revival was witnessed. Those who promote the primacy of preaching as a militant creed are often strong champions of the sovereignty of God. There seems to be a tension between promoting his sovereignty and confining his Spirit's 'unction' to the sermon.

A prayer ministry model has been the dominant one within this time of refreshing. It will help clarify issues if we examine the Toronto Vineyard model and the wider Vineyard perspective in terms of prayer ministry.

A prayer model

The Pentecostal/charismatic wing of evangelicalism has often been dominated in the past by the 'mighty man' philosophy of ministry. A man or a woman who had 'died to self', lived a life of holiness and hungered and thirsted after God, might become endued with a powerful 'anointing'. The Holy Spirit could move more powerfully through them because they had been 'called' to a miracle ministry. There are still vestiges of this perspective in the ministry of Rodney Howard-Browne, as we noted in the last chapter.

The charismatic movement of recent times has placed a great value on the priesthood of all believers. The Vineyard conferences of the eighties were a revolution for many in that, following a biblical presentation of a given subject, the delegates, joined occasionally by Vineyard team members, would be invited to pray for each other. Vineyard leader John Wimber believed 'that we can all minister in the power of the Spirit'. This did not mean that the issues of holiness, personal surrender to God and spiritual hunger were neglected, just that you didn't have to be a 'superstar' to be used by God. However, pastors at the conferences would still sometimes sit at the end of rows to weed out any freelance cranks who might zero in on their people.

There was also a growing recognition that careful guidelines for prophecy and care about the spiritual and emotional maturity of those involved in counselling was vital if a newfound freedom was not to be abused.

This 'mighty people' ethos naturally infused the practice of the Airport Vineyard as they found their January time of blessing beginning to flow into weeks and months of renewal.

Given that so many were receiving prayer they would stack all the chairs after the sermon and after a short time of worship their ministry team would begin to pray for people. The 'team' ethos was pursued for two reasons. The church wanted to be accountable for the ministry taking place. It also meant that the rest of the congregation could concentrate primarily on listening and receiving – not a common experience for many of the leaders, who were often busy 'givers' rather than relaxed 'receivers'.

Many fell down and the ministry team often needed 'catchers' to prevent people falling on each other or hurting themselves. This practice has provoked some internal dialogue within the Vineyard movement. John Wimber is not militantly against 'catchers' but he is wary 'that it focuses the phenomena of the Spirit primarily on the issue of falling and whatever would occur in the aftermath'.

Writing in *Vineyard Reflections* he encourages leaders to ensure that 'catchers' are not passive, and are participating in the prayer. He suggests that where possible people should be prayed for within the normal seating arrangements.

The Airport Vineyard, Elli Mumford, Bishop David Pytches and many others repeatedly remind people that the phenomena are secondary to the fruit. Terry Virgo encourages people to 'tell not only about the phenomena experienced but also about the inward change that the experience has led to'.

Wimber is quite emphatic: 'I've called these "seeker meetings". By that I'm simply referring to Christians who are seeking more of the presence and work of God in their lives. Those meetings ought to be characterised by messages that are Christ-centred, and altar calls that are Christ-centred, as opposed to phenomena-centred. In my opinion, it is not valid to invite people forward simply to shake, fall, laugh or cry. The phenomena are not the issue. The issue is the impact of the presence of God on the individual's life and the growth of godly character in the aftermath.'

God confronted Paul on the road to Damascus. He also inspired him to write 'work out your salvation' and 'study to show yourself approved'. Wimber, like many of his contemporaries, doesn't believe in putting 'crisis' sanctification against 'progressive' sanctification or growth in Christian maturity. He comments:

> Our theology and experience of revival must be tempered by our understanding of sanctification. Sanctification is the necessary counterpart to justification, or the forgiveness of sins.
>
> Sanctification is that work of the Holy Spirit that takes place both as 'a one-time act, valid for all time, imputing and imparting holiness, and as an ongoing, progressive work' (*New Dictionary of Theology*, p. 615). In the sense that it's ongoing, we co-operate with the Holy Spirit.
>
> All Christians need to be cleansed and dedicated to the service of God (Rom 12:1-2) and thereby make practical our prayer, 'Your kingdom come, your will be done on earth (and in my life) as it is in heaven.'
>
> Let us not allow ourselves to equate the experience of various manifestations of the Spirit with sanctification. Such experiences may accompany, accent, or provide a milestone on the journey of sanctification, but they are not necessarily the agents of sanctification.

Charles Finney was clear about the place of phenomena:

> We need fear no kind of degree of excitement which is pro-
> duced simply by perceived truth, and is consistent with the
> healthy operation of the intellectual powers. Whatever exceeds
> this must be disastrous. In general, those cases of bodily pros-
> tration of which I have spoken occur without the apparent inter-
> vention of any external means adapted to produce such a
> result. . . the excitement produced when the Holy Ghost reveals
> God to the soul. . . is not only consistent with the clearest and
> most enlarged perceptions of the intelligence, but directly pro-
> motes and produces such perceptions. Indeed, it promotes the
> free and unembarrassed action of both the intelligence and the
> will.
>
> Now it appears to me of great importance to distinguish in
> these cases between things that differ. When I see cases of
> extraordinary excitement, I have learned to inquire as calmly
> and affectionately as I can into the views of truth taken by the
> mind at the time. I can then judge of its character. If it really
> originates in clear views by the Holy Ghost, of the character of
> God and of the great truths of His government, the mind will be
> full of these truths and will spontaneously give them off when-
> ever there is an ability to utter them. . . But where the attention
> seems to be occupied with one's own feelings, and when they
> can give no intelligible reason for feeling as they do, very little
> confidence can be placed in their state. (*Reflections on Revival*,
> pp 49-51.)

The infilling of the Holy Spirit

Orthodox Christian belief is that the Christian is indwelt by
the Holy Spirit at the moment of conversion. This 'posi-
tional' filling will sometimes be supplemented by an 'experiential' filling whereby the believer may receive a 'grace
gift' or 'charism', a special touch of the Holy Spirit to undertake a specific act, such as prayer for healing, tongues,
prophecy, a word of knowledge or any type of supernatural
gift.

This experiential 'filling' can be seen in the life of Moses. In Numbers 11:25 it tells us that the Lord took of the Spirit resting on Moses and distributed it on the seventy elders who, when it rested on them, prophesied. Moses told Joshua that he wished the Lord would put his Spirit on all God's people so that they could all be prophets.

Saul, King of Israel, had a similar experience when the Spirit of the Lord came upon him in power. He was to prophesy and the promise was that he would be a changed person (1 Sam 10:5-10).

This is further amplified in Rodney Howard-Browne's understanding of the anointing of the Holy Spirit, explained in Chapter 6. He takes the words of Jesus in John 4 and suggests that the indwelling of the Spirit is like a well. 'Everyone who drinks this water will be thirsty again, but whoever drinks the water I give him will never thirst. Indeed the water I give him will become in him a spring of water welling up to eternal life' (Jn 4:13-14).

While we may be sustained by the 'well', Howard-Browne believes that a 'river' of the Holy Spirit will flow out from us. We discover this river imagery in John 7: 37-39:

> On the last and greatest day of the Feast, Jesus stood and said in a loud voice, 'If anyone is thirsty, let him come to me and drink. Whoever believes in me, as the Scripture has said, streams of living water will flow from within him.' By this he meant the Spirit, whom those who believed in him were later to receive. Up to that time the Spirit had not been given, since Jesus had not yet been glorified.

As we pray for each other there may well be a transference of the 'river' of the Holy Spirit. Just as God took his Spirit that was on Moses and distributed it among the seventy elders, so Paul passed the 'anointing of the Spirit' to Timothy. 'Do not neglect your gift, which was given you through a prophetic message when the body of elders laid their hands on you' (1 Tim 4:14). 'For this reason I remind you to fan into flame the gift of God, which is in you through the laying on of my hands. For God did not give us a spirit of timidity, but a spirit of power, of love and of self-discipline' (2 Tim 1:6).

The river metaphor is also applicable when talk turns to the 'tangible presence'. God is omnipresent, ie everywhere, but there may be times when we can see, hear or feel his presence. Sometimes he reveals something of his glory, as he did to Moses, or sometimes he comes 'down in the cloud' (Num 11:25).

His presence is therefore both internal and external. His external presence is symbolised by Ezekiel's vision of the river flowing from the Temple (Ez 47:1-12), bringing life and healing wherever it goes. His internal presence is referred to in Ephesians 5:18: 'Do not get drunk on wine, which leads to debauchery. Instead be filled with the Spirit.'

The original Greek words mean 'be being filled'. It is a continuous process. Why do we need this? C.H.Spurgeon answered, 'Because I leak.' The encouragement to drink afresh of the Spirit is common at this time.

The reasons why people are eager to receive prayer or a touch from God are many. Some are symbolically 'tarrying in Jerusalem', just as the disciples did, waiting for a fresh infilling of the Holy Spirit, so that they may have a new power for service. Some, sensitive to the reality that they are distant from God despite their profession of faith, are taking the first steps towards reorienting their lifestyle so that their spiritual indifference is shattered and the Holy Spirit can have free reign in their thought lives and their subsequent actions.

Some, as they enter meetings where God makes himself manifest, find themselves challenged, touched by conviction, released into joy or whatever. This can happen after personal prayer, sometimes after a corporate prayer such as 'Father God, for the sake of Jesus, send your Holy Spirit', and sometimes without prayer.

When people's hearts are turned towards God and they are seeking change in their life through co-operation with the Holy Spirit, it is likely that he may have to 'clean up the house' so that he can work more effectively. For others there may simply be new insights and revelations from him.

It is at this time that the physical phenomena may be witnessed. As people 'soak', or 'tarry' or are crying out for 'more' then God sends his Spirit to equip and renew his hungry, thirsty people.

Sitting or standing, prostrate or praying, people may be overcome by a variety of phenomena. What are these phenomena? Are there any indicators in Scripture in respect of them? Have they happened in history?

It needs to be stressed that phenomena only mean that God might be working in a life. Jonathan Edwards comments: '. . .a work is not to be judged of by any effects on the bodies of men, such as tears, tremblings, groans, loud outcries, agonies of bodies, or the failing of bodily strength. The influence persons are under is not to be judged of one way or other by such effects on the body; and the reason is because the Scripture nowhere gives us any such rule.'

Writing in *Revival of Religion*, Edwards reiterated this point. 'Some that have had very great raptures of joy and have been extraordinarily filled and have had their bodies overcome, and that very often, but have manifested far less of the temper of Christians in their conduct since than some others that have been still and have made no great outward show. But then again, there are many others that have had extraordinary joys and emotions of mind, with frequent great effects upon their bodies that behave themselves steadfastly, as humble, amiable, eminent Christians.'

The possibility that we might be touched bodily seems quite clear in Jeremiah 23:9: 'Concerning the prophets: My heart is broken within me; all my bones tremble. I am like a drunken man, like a man overcome by wine, because of the Lord and his holy words.'

Justin Dennison, pastor of Bramlea Baptist, a Toronto church near the Vineyard reflecting on the phenomena in a letter to fellow Baptist ministers, suggests, 'It would seem therefore not inappropriate to at least accept what Scripture does not forbid and church history seems to support.'

The phenomena of revival/renewal

Falling

The most widely acknowledged and commonly seen physical response at many churches in recent months has been people falling to the floor. I would suggest that there are six reasons why this might happen.

1. Stricken by the Spirit, people feel their bodily energy dissolve and cannot stand any longer. They may fall into a trance-like state.
2. People feel unsteady for a variety of reasons. Wary of analysing away every potential touch of God, they allow themselves to crumple to the floor and rest.
3. The existence of a surrender/vulnerability motif in the testimony of many suggests that voluntary prostration signifies an attitude of surrender and openness to God. While they rest, they may remain conscious, but in a prayer or in a day-dream state. Some who are not 'stricken' have had profound visionary experiences while resting and being prayed for or engaged in personal prayer or meditation.
4. Some are pushed. For this reason there are those who will not put their hands on a person's head or touch them in a way that could infer that pressure was being exerted.

   Those who push are guilty of a 'ministry of manifestations'. You may find that they preach the manifestations rather than a message that draws the heart towards Christ.

In their misplaced zeal, or out of a need to authenticate their ministry, they stage 'demonstrations' of God's power, unrelated to any contentful preaching or explanation or even the explicit desire of those pushed to be prayed for. They may justify their action as 'faith building' and insist that the 'anointing' knocks people over, not their hand.

These people can cause deep disillusionment and discredit a genuine work of God. God will chide the immature and eventually remove the 'fakers' because they cause people to stumble – literally and figuratively.

5. Some fall because of implicit peer pressure. They don't want to be seen to resist God's workings. It's an understandable reaction, but it is not helpful in the long term. A wise pastor will ensure that people know that 'falling' is not a spiritual badge. We need to pray for people in a variety of settings – sitting, standing, prostrate – to clarify that the essential goal is an encounter with God, not a 'traditional' physical response.

6. Some who fall or writhe are attention seekers, tares among the wheat. They may be insecure or highly emotional and conditioned towards behaviour that causes them to be the centre of attention.

Weeping

This is of course the acceptable phenomenon. You'll hear few people speak against it. In the days of Nehemiah the people cried as they heard the word of the Lord read to them. Nehemiah encouraged them not to weep – there was definitely no auto-suggestion here. He encouraged them to go and celebrate with great joy.

William Williams writing in *The Experience Meeting* of a prayer meeting in 1762 in Wales, recalls, 'Now some were weeping, some praying, some singing. . . and all full of wonder at and love and amazement at the Lord's work.'

People may weep for a variety of reasons – sorrow over

sin and a compassion for the lost and broken are just two.

Laughter

This phenomenon has been the most remarked on in recent days. In Psalm 126 it speaks of a people whose mouths were full of laughter. The writer of Ecclesiastes notes that there is a time to weep and a time to laugh. (Quite when one would laugh in some contemporary churches is debatable.)

William Williams, speaking of the same meeting mentioned above, talks of 'some. . . filled with heavenly laughter'.

The phenomenon is by no means new. Watchman Nee encountered it and felt constrained to denounce it.

Jonathan Edwards notes that those touched by a sense of grace were overcome by a 'joyful surprise [which] caused their hearts, as it were, to leap so that they have been ready to break forth into laughter'.

Perhaps some feel for the first time that God has given them permission to enjoy their faith, not just endure the attacks of the devil and hope for heaven.

Trance-like states/visionary experiences

These are not uncommon in Scripture. Paul tells how God used one to warn him: 'When I returned to Jerusalem and was praying at the temple, I fell into a trance and saw the Lord speaking. "Quick!" he said to me. "Leave Jerusalem immediately, because they will not accept your testimony about me."'

Peter also had a trance experience associated with prayer (Acts 10:10-23). God used the trance to change Peter's mind about the Gentiles. It was a mystical experience but it had a profound effect on Peter's intellectual understanding of God's purpose, particularly as God was prompting a Gentile at the same time via an angelic visitor to seek out Peter.

All these types of experience should be weighed and tested, as conventional prophecy would be, to ensure that they reflect broad biblical orthodoxy. (Several examples are recounted elsewhere in this book.)

Some, while in these trance-like states, may enact what they are 'dreaming' of. These actions may include 'running' or 'swimming'.

Shaking

In Jeremiah 5:22 God asks, 'Should you not tremble in my presence?' When Daniel experienced one of his visions, those with him did not see the vision, but felt the presence of God and were deeply affected (Dan 10:1-11).

God told Isaiah that he would esteem those who 'tremble at his word' (Is 66:2).

George Fox, founder of the Quakers, saw great conviction fall upon people to whom he preached. 'The Lord's power began to shake them,' he says, 'and great meetings we began to have, and a mighty power and work of God there was amongst people.'

Prostration

There are several biblical references noted by Bill Jackson in *What in the World is Happening to Us?*:

> The most common phenomenon we have seen in our meetings is people falling down. Often they remain conscious but engage with the Lord. They feel weak and find it difficult to do anything but rest with God. We have seen that as they lie with the Lord, they have had significant changes in their lives. This is all well and good, but is there any biblical precedent for this?
>
> Genesis 15:12: 'Abram fell into a deep sleep and a thick, dreadful darkness came over him.' This literally reads, 'a deep sleep fell on Abram.' The Hebrew word radam means to be in or fall into a deep sleep. This is the same word that is used when God put Adam to sleep when he made Eve (Gen 2:21).
>
> 1 Samuel 19: 'Saul walked along prophesying. . . he stripped off his robes and also prophesied in Samuel's presence. He lay that way all that day and night This is why people say, "Is Saul

also among the prophets?"' This text shows that for something close to a twenty-four-hour period Saul lay in a prone position with God speaking through him.

Ezekiel 3:23: '. . . And the glory of the Lord was standing there, like the glory I had seen by the Kebar river, and I fell face down.'

Daniel 8:17: 'As he (Gabriel) came near. . . I was terrified and fell on my face.'

Daniel 10:9: In another divine encounter with an angelic being Daniel says, 'When I heard the sound of his words I then was lying stunned (radam) on the ground.'

John 18:6: As Judas and the soldiers came to arrest Jesus, they had an interesting encounter. When Jesus said, 'I am he,' they jumped back, and fell to the ground. Here we see an immediate falling back in response to the presence of Jesus. They were apparently able to get up shortly thereafter because they went on to arrest Jesus.

Acts 9:22-26: When Paul was apprehended on the road to Damascus by a light from heaven he says, 'I fell to the ground and heard a voice.' Again we see that falling was a normal response to a divine visitation.

Revelation 1:17: In the visionary experience that resulted in the book of Revelation, John, speaking of his angelic encounter, says, 'When I saw him I fell at his feet as though dead.' Here we see an experience similar to Adam's and Abram's where the person not only falls but is also unconscious for an extended period of time.

Jonathan Edwards, the main instrument and theologian of the Great Awakening in America (1725-1760), says in his *Account of the Revival of Religion in Northampton 1740-1742*:

Many have had their religious affections raised far beyond what they had ever been before; and there were some instances of persons lying in a sort of trance, remaining perhaps for a whole twenty-four hours motionless, and with their senses locked up; but in the meantime under strong imaginations, as though they went to heaven and had there a vision of glorious and delightful objects.

It was a very frequent thing to see outcries, faintings, convulsions, and such like, both with distress, and also admiration and joy.

It was not the manner here to hold meetings all night, nor was it common to continue them till very late in the night; but it was pretty often that there were some so affected, and their bodies so overcome, that they could not go home, but were obligated to stay all night where they were.

Charles Finney (1792-1875) was one of the most powerful revivalists since the reformation. One description of his ministry reads:

At a country place named Sodom, in the state of New York, Finney gave one address in which he described the condition of Sodom before God destroyed it. 'I had not spoken in this strain more than a quarter of an hour,' says he, 'when an awful solemnity seemed to settle upon them; the congregation began to fall from their seats in every direction, and cried for mercy. If I had had a sword in each hand, I could not have cut them down as fast as they fell. Nearly the whole congregation were either on their knees or prostrate, I should think, in less than two minutes from the shock that fell upon them. Every one prayed who was able to speak at all.' Similar scenes were witnessed in many other places.

Drunkenness

Jeremiah said that he was like a drunken man overcome by wine because of the Lord and his holy words (Jer 23:9). The disciples on the day of Pentecost were accused of drunkenness. Eli also accused Hannah of being drunk (1 Sam 1:13). Saul, prophesying before Samuel, removed all his robes and lay down for the best part of twenty-four hours, prophesying all the while. That must have looked remarkably like drunkenness.

There are widespread reports of this phenomenon in Argentina, America, Canada and in recent times in the

British Isles. Reports from the 1859 Ulster revival describing occasions when people were carried home and had to rest in bed, often in a trance-like state and experiencing powerful visions could indicate a similar phenomenon.

For those who are prone to be influenced by the 'flesh and the devil', there may be temptations in this phenomenon that can lead to a pseudo-drunkenness and what church leader Terry Virgo describes as 'unhelpful foolishness'.

Jerking

This is quite common at the Airport Vineyard and in some of the mainstream, thoughtful churches where there has been an openness to the move of God. It has no biblical precedent, but plenty of historical precedent among twentieth-century Pentecostals, particularly in the Pentecostal Holiness denomination.

Some talk of an experience of the Holy Spirit coming on or over them in waves that are experienced physically. One can literally fell 'jarred'.

Rolling

Some will roll back and forth across the floor. This was a phenomenon that particularly upset Jessie Penn Lewis, who despite her early championing of the 1904 Welsh revival in *The Life of Faith*, later vigorously criticised aspects of it in *War on the Saints*. Many feel that she was too ready to attribute works of the flesh to the devil.

Jumping

The biblical picture of the healed beggar, walking and leaping and praising God, is perhaps helpful here.

The practice was often common in Welsh revival over the centuries. Wesley was wary. He didn't write off those involved, but he felt it was a distraction. Others were not so negative. Gilbert Egerton writing in *Flame of God* reports: 'The practice of jumping in response to the word being preached began in 1762 and persisted well into the last century in many parts of Wales. In order to distinguish them from their English counterparts, they became known as the "Welsh jumpers". It is probably true that the majority of "jumpers" were Calvinistic Methodist, but not all. The practice spread to other denominations as they too became imbued with the spirit of Methodism.'

A fascinating glimpse of the practice is afforded by John Lewis in 1851 and mentioned in E. Roberts' *Revival and Its Fruit*:

> Such excitement, such jumping and exulting, I never saw either before or since! Old men and old women clasping each other's hands and leaping like roe deer. . . I can offer no explanation for this except that the new nature in them must have been drawing them upwards in a most powerful manner. I have seen praise before this and after this, but jumping and leaping only this once. Oh! What a relief for thousands to give vent to the spiritual energy which was in their breasts. Some weeping, some singing; others exulting and very many doing this while 'leaping and praising God'. This was a meeting to be remembered forever.

When eighteenth-century Welsh revivalist Daniel Rowland was being urged by John Thornton, a rich Englishman, to condemn the practice of jumping, he replied, 'You English speak against us and say, "Jumpers, jumpers!" But we Welsh must justly say of you "Sleepers, sleepers!"'

Animal noises

A careful study of historical revival will unearth references to roaring on several occasions. No particular explanation is offered, but context would suggest that these were regarded as the cries of tormented souls.

Within the contemporary charismatic movement such noises would normally spark a deliverance session as a demonic source would be assumed.

The practice arose in Toronto in recent times and has particularly affected leaders, such as Bishop David Pytches and a leading Canadian pastor called Daniel Chui.

Marc Dupont told *Alpha* magazine:

> I feel that God wants to remind us that as well as Christ being the Lamb of God, he is the Lion of Judah. It says in Amos 3:8, 'When the lion roars who will not fear; when God speaks who cannot but prophesy?'
>
> I was meeting recently with eight or nine pastors from Vancouver Island. God touched them and they fell on the floor shaking. Daniel Chui, a Vancouver-based Cantonese Chinese with a multinational Pentecostal church, began to roar like a lion. The normal rule of thumb would be that he needed deliverance. I felt God tell me that this was symbolic. The dragon is highly symbolic in Chinese culture. This symbolic prophetic act signifies that the Lion of Judah will triumph. It mainly happens to two types of people. First, leaders who have trans-denominational ministries that God will be using for works of unity. Second, those who are seriously called to intercessory prayer – for churches, cities and nations.

Those experiencing the roaring phenomenon also appeal to Hosea 11:10: 'They will follow the Lord; he will roar like a lion. When he roars his children will come trembling from the west.'

The phenomenon is regarded therefore as a prophetic symbol and Airport Vineyard leaders will urge those involved to prophesy in their own language following the symbolic action. Indiscriminate roaring is not encouraged, although it seems to occur that way in some meetings where there is not an appropriate level of leadership.

Other animal noises manifest in meetings can provoke an after-meeting rush for the concordance to seek positive biblical examples of what the animal symbolises. Critics seek out negative references and a battle of textual references begins. The texts usually balance each other out!

John Wimber, the international leader of the Vineyard

movement, is very positive about the Toronto Vineyard, but seems to feel that this particular phenomenon is not particularly significant.

Church Times journalist Colin Moreton broached the subject in a feature 'Making Room for a Visit from God' (30th September 1994):

> We wondered why God should make people bark and bleat and roar and produce other zoological noises. 'To attempt to answer that is to attempt to answer the unanswerable. There's nothing in scripture that supports this kind of phenomena. I know of no major principle in the history of the church that ever said, "that means this." I feel no obligation to try to explain it. It's just phenomena, it's just people responding to God.'

> Some critics had suggested they were rather responding to each other, in a state of heightened emotion. John Wimber said: 'I have no inclination to try to answer the average sceptical onlooker. I'm not a sceptic, I am a Christian, and I believe in preaching the word of God and ministering through the power and presence of the Spirit. I think this reaction is just a reaction, and I don't see much difference between that and soccer fans making all the strange and exotic noises they make when they get excited. Nor do I see it as something that ought to be endorsed, embraced, affirmed or accepted by the Church. I think we ought to ignore it.'

Spirit fire and wildfire

Jack Deere, in *Surprised by the Power of the Spirit* (Kingsway), cautions those in leadership to be careful:

> If we attach great significance to the manifestations, people will equate the manifestations with the work of the Spirit and even view them as a badge of spirituality. When that happens, insecure people will often imitate these manifestations to draw attention to themselves and to appear spiritual.

> An equally significant mistake would be to try to suppress the manifestations. Imagine a person who is under such intense

conviction by the Holy Spirit for his sins that he has an acute sense of the torments of hell and is trembling as a result of that conviction.

Now imagine the immense folly of approaching a person like that and telling him to snap out of it! If we attempt to suppress a real physical manifestation of the Holy Spirit's work, we are in danger of putting out the fire of the Spirit.

There is care among many therefore to be sensitive even when bringing correction. John Arnott will encourage people to concentrate on the sermon, or remind those involved that the spirit of the prophet is subject to the prophet.

Terry Virgo's home church in Columbia, USA has set aside a room where people can go or be taken and receive prayer or continue to be touched by God, without disturbing the main meeting.

In some instances the leadership will simply call for quiet or pray that God will silence that which is not of him and calm the rest. This general type of prayer was used at one convention where, despite their sympathy for what was currently happening, the leaders felt that the disruption of the sermon couldn't continue. The prayer was effective.

On a practical note, it may help to consider not always praying for people prior to the sermon, as has become the practice. The manifestations may not put the preacher off, but newcomers tend to gawk, and those inclined to emotionalism may feel they have 'permission' to interrupt.

Many of the manifestations are not necessarily associated with the prayer ministry time however. Pastors will need to ask God for the wisdom of Solomon and the patience of Job. Our attempt to ensure that wildfire doesn't take over from Spirit fire should be tempered with the realisation that people must be given 'permission' to be emotional and cry or laugh or shout their praises.

Explain, explain, explain

It is vital that we help our congregational Bereans and those simply shocked by the new and the different and that we seek to remind people of appropriate scriptures. We must place all the phenomena in the wider context of the overall purposes of God in personal salvation and restoration, prayer and intercession and evangelism.

People need the security of calm leadership in the midst of change and innovation.

The prophetic impulse/God-encounter tension

This book does not attempt to explore the psychological dynamics possibly at work. There are two underlying schools of thought, nevertheless. One suggestion is that the phenomena are a human reaction to a divine touch; the other is that a person is overwhelmed by God and the manifestations may be involuntary.

I personally lean towards both views as being legitimate, albeit in different circumstances. The Bible seems to indicate that sometimes we can choose whether or not to express that which God has prompted us to think or the emotion he has unlocked. The injunction in 1 Corinthians 14 that the spirit of the prophet is subject to the prophet would seem to point in this direction.

However, there would seem to be evidence in Scripture that there were occasions when people were completely overcome by the Spirit. We have already noted that Saul and his companions had the Spirit come upon them and cause them to prophesy, and that those attacking Jesus fell back under the power of the Spirit (Jn 18:6). There was an exterior expression of the Spirit when tongues of fire appeared on the day of Pentecost and touched all the disciples.

The revelatory vision experiences where people are confronted with their own sin are another example of God invading our reality, not merely prompting our thought life.

Careful balance is needed here. Too much emphasis on the phenomena always being the human expression of the divine prompting can lead us to a slow rationalisation of the supernatural. Too much emphasis on God overcoming us with phenomena can lead to a superspirituality which forgets that not every emotional impulse is from God.

Ministering to those who remain untouched

It's important to clarify what we mean by 'untouched'. Some will feel untouched because they haven't had a powerful physical 'validating' experience.

They may however have been touched emotionally through tears, or a feeling of well-being and joy. Others may simply have been provoked to think more biblically or simply encouraged by seeing others being built up in the faith.

In fact a willingness to be encouraged by what has happened to everyone else is vital, and helps our congregation members move away from an individualistic Western mindset where personal fulfilment is the dominating goal rather than a commitment to God and his people.

Some are physically untouched but are used powerfully to bless others. One leaders' guidance note currently in circulation states that one man, who spent twelve hours in high-powered meetings with no overt physical reactions, is now among the leaders of what is happening in the UK.

Marc Dupont, powerfully used within the Airport Vineyard and around the world, has not fallen over, laughed or had any extreme physical reaction throughout the entire period of renewal since January 1994.

The Champaign Vineyard ministry notes remind pastors that they should 'keep reassuring people that it's OK if they do not manifest anything unusual when they receive prayer. God works differently in different people. Remember to encourage people that it's not manifestations we are after but changed hearts. The manifestations are simply a by-product.'

We may however need to be aware of significant barriers to people receiving from God. These tend to centre around three specific areas, addressed by Airport Vineyard pastor John Arnott in a talk he gives to people seeking to make sense of their own reactions to the Airport meetings.

He counsels people to 'hang onto your common sense' and tells of his own struggle with the issue of falling down, and his tendency to rationalise everything. He identifies control, fear and analysis as stumbling blocks for those willing to receive from God. What follows includes personal insights from myself as well as material from John.

Control

For many pastors, the pastoral mindset is difficult to set aside. They are over-alert, watching the meeting, anticipating what is going to happen next. They are reluctant to be vulnerable, regarding themselves as an example to the congregation, and loath to be in any situation where weakness might be exposed. (That's why they have to get blessed somewhere else – like Toronto.)

Fear

We fear deception, we fear emotion, we fear Satan. Trust, born from 'hanging on to our common sense' and evaluating the spiritual stance of those whose meetings we attend, can take us past the fear-of-deception hurdle.

A biblical understanding of the proper role of emotion in spiritual experience, namely as a fruit of understanding, will help us avoid emotionalism but steer us away from 'Spock' Christianity, where like the *Star Trek* character we are all intellect and no emotion.

With respect to fear of Satan, John warms to his subject: 'We need to have more faith in God's ability to bless us than in Satan's ability to deceive us.'

For those who fret over an unhelpful 'transference' if they

are prayed for by the immature or by 'demonised' people, John offers the following: 'The Holy Spirit is in your life, trust him. There's not a perfect person alive on the earth.' He's not insensitive to the idea that the immature can cause harm – that's why Vineyard have an accountability structure in the ministry team – but he's wary of a restrictive attitude grounded in fear.

Analysis

John Arnott uses the analogy of affection and encourages people not to clinically analyse their experience with God. He urges 'common sense' and is quite clear that he is not interested in being involved in something that is 'flaky'.

For myself I find that some of my most profound spiritual experiences happen when I'm in a day-dreaming state. My mind has not shut off, but I have often disassociated myself from my immediate surroundings. I'm not 'on guard', but I am not in a mindless ecstasy either.

There is a proper place for analysis – the Berean believers are an example – but there is also a place for unself-conscious adoration and focusing on God. For some this may mean ceasing to strive to work up an emotion according to formula. People being prayed for should be encouraged to be calm and rested, not praying in English or a prayer language.

Let's leave the final word on the phenomena with John Wimber. He made his point very clear in an interview with the *Church Times* (30th September 1994):

> Let's not lift up phenomena. This isn't about phenomena, this is about God visiting the church. Let's talk about God, let's teach the main things of scripture, and let's focus this experience on the works of God. Therefore, let's go feed the hungry and care for the broken and the bruised in the community, let's look after widows and divorcees and the fatherless, and let's preach the gospel to the lost.

9

Questions People Ask

I have sought to give a broad overview of the phenomena of revival. For many people questions still remain. What are those questions and are there helpful responses?

I have heard it said in meetings that we shouldn't analyse – just receive.

There is a tension here between two different aspects of our relationship with God. If we take the analogy of marriage, we believe that a wise man or woman carefully considers their prospective partner: Do they have mutual interests, similar goals in life, compatible temperaments? This analysis, in the midst of romantic idealism and physical attraction is wise – it denotes an open-minded but careful person.

Having made careful preparation, however, once the 'marriage' has taken place it's not always helpful to analyse every aspect of a relationship. We are swept up in emotion and attraction.

Similarly we will sometimes find ourselves caught up in unself-conscious worship, or a focus on Jesus in prayer. This focus may precipitate quite profound spiritual encounters. That doesn't require watchfulness – it requires release and passion. Our moral, spiritual, biblical, intellectual framework remains as a 'hedge' to guard against that which is unhelpful, intruding, but we trust God to bless us through his Spirit.

We need to affirm both the wisdom of the Bereans and the reality of some of our emotional spiritual experience. Sometimes faith and growth are not simply a matter of logical progression of thought, but involve us being carried away 'to the third heaven' as Paul was.

Quiet laughter might be of the Holy Spirit, but surely not hysterical laughter?

There are all kinds of laughter in the Bible. Released captives found their mouths full of laughter (Ps 126); elsewhere laughter was a means of mocking or scorn.

Setting aside questions of the appropriateness of laughter during various parts of the service, such as the sermon or the Bible reading, the question of discerning which types of laughter in a meeting are of the Holy Spirit and which are not, is a subjective, legalistic minefield. What do we know of the character of the person concerned? What fruit do we subsequently see in their lives? These are better criteria than our highly subjective opinions.

Don't New Age groups and occultists promote their deceptions with the use of group laughter, laughter therapy, long singing sessions, trance states and other things that we see in charismatic meetings?

If the Bible suggests that God may cause people to tremble, fall to the floor, be overcome by the Spirit or have mystical dreams, then it matters not that counterfeit religion may mimic both the means and the effects by which Christians focus on and receive from God.

God's primary interest is in our religious behaviour and the conformity of our lives to his standards of ethical holiness. If his good gifts of music, emotion and biblically mandated actions such as the laying on of hands can bring about those ends and cause us to hear and receive from the Spirit, then God is pleased.

In the worship of Nebuchadnezzar and his idol a set of musical instruments was used. The same instruments are mentioned in Psalm 149 as part of an explicit command about worship. There was nothing intrinsically good or evil in the instruments themselves – only in the purposes for which they were employed.

Any aspect of creation can be used or abused. The fact that people use and abuse emotion, music, oratorical skills and the like does not disqualify them from their created purpose. Guilt by association is deeply unhelpful.

Why do people have to go to Toronto to 'catch it'? Doesn't the Holy Spirit 'spontaneously combust' when he comes in power?

Timothy caught something of an additional empowerment from Paul. God gave the seventy elders some of the Spirit that had rested on Moses. The disciples 'tarried in Jerusalem'.

Those who travel to a place of revival are 'tarrying in Jerusalem' to receive a new empowerment and a 'Paul/ Timothy' impartation from those already touched.

Two of Moses' elders were not at the meeting we read of in Numbers 11. The Spirit still rested on them and they too prophesied. Some were infected, others just caught the fire. God it seems isn't interested in our either/or mentality, but often works in a both/and way. In earlier chapters we have heard of churches touched by God before any contact with Rodney Howard-Browne, the Airport Vineyard or any other centre of renewal.

Aren't people just doing things they have heard suggested by the preacher?

Paul Reid of Christian Fellowship Church in Belfast saw one third of the people in a meeting overtaken by the Spirit. He hadn't mentioned phenomena. Ken and Lois Gott and Gerald Coates studiously avoided mentioning the phenomena to their congregations but saw them break out nevertheless.

The experience of Trowbridge minister John Darling is recounted in a letter to Holy Trinity Brompton's news sheet:

> The evening started with a time of worship, and while we were singing one of our members shot out of the room. I followed her, thinking she was upset, to find her doubled up with laughter. She had fled the room thinking that was the polite thing to do. I had planned to explain in my talk what God is doing in this release of joy, but I hadn't reached that point. I explained briefly to her and encouraged her to rejoin the others.
>
> As we came back it was obvious that others were being touched, all before any mention of the experience.

Some advance a theory of 'hypnotic induction'. A crowd, concentrating on the words and gestures of a speaker, can, it is said, be induced to an action promoted by the speaker, and with their rational detachment suspended, become involved without thinking in that activity.

This is not the place for a detailed overview of hypnosis. Suffice it to say that people are always free to leave Christian meetings. Many, from habit, carefully evaluate what they are hearing.

One also wonders where a vigorous promotion of this theory would leave some of the key biblical characters. Was Peter right, in the heightened atmosphere of the situation of apparent drunkenness and unusual language gifts being used, to call the Jews to repent and believe (Acts 2)? He would probably be accused of inductive hypnosis today.

Christians have to walk the tightrope of the interplay between their rational mind and their emotions. Despising either makes us unbiblical. God created them both. If a call to repentance challenges the mind and also causes the emotions of conviction, sorrow and regret that hasten change, then let's welcome it.

Aren't many of the people in these meetings self-indulgent blessing hunters? The ones I've met are.

There are some. There's always a certain number of spiritual nomads running around 'chasing the glory'. The testimonies in this book, however, are from people committed to building mature local church congregations. They want to see Jesus exalted and thoughtful Christianity advanced.

'Let those who are without carnal Christians somewhere in their congregation cast the first stone' might be an applicable paraphrase here.

Just because something is in the Bible doesn't mean it's the normal experience of every Christian, does it?

One prominent writer tells us that Paul's Damascus Road experience 'is hardly a normative experience for all believers'. But many believers, whether the writer likes it or not, tend to have literal or visionary experiences of a similar nature. The biblical references to falling forwards, backwards or other physical reactions do not mean that we are all required to have these experiences. They don't prove anything per se. But to suggest that all our physical reactions to a divine encounter must correspond exactly to proof-text criteria is to turn the Bible from the story of salvation and grace into the rule book of salvation.

There's no foundation of repentance in this so-called 'time of refreshing'. That can't be right, can it?

Please read Chapter 4 of this book. . . And don't believe

what you read in the mainstream press. They only tell you the 'surface' story.

Perhaps the devil will cause counterfeit 'fruit' to follow counterfeit signs and wonders produced by false Christs and false prophets. How can we tell?

There may be false signs and wonders, and even legalistic holiness, among those who are deceived by cults and spiritual impostors, but the real fruit will always emerge as a verification of the genuine, biblically-oriented work of God in a person's life. Why would the devil exalt Jesus? Martyn Lloyd-Jones comments: 'Here is a church that is in a period of dryness and drought, why should the devil suddenly do something which calls attention to religion and Jesus?. . . If this is the work of the devil, then the devil is an unutterable fool.'

This blessing is divisive – how can it be of God?

Division often arises out of impatience and judgementalism, both from those who are against a new expression of God's power, and from those who are immature in their expression of enthusiasm for it.

Mature believers will respect each other's dignity and will disagree agreeably. Moderation is much more likely to spring from loving, careful but honest dialogue than from a 'heresy, deception, doom and gloom' mentality.

It was divisive when Paul took a stand against the legalism of the Judeans, but he still had to do it and to act as God commanded. Division over principle is unavoidable in our fallen state. Party spirit and division over wrong attitudes, however, should be anathema to any believer sensitive to the Spirit.

What we need is 'ministry in the Spirit', not these emotional physical reactions. Surely God is spirit and that's how he works?

This sounds very spiritual, but it's a shorthand way of saying that God works only in a fairly calm, intellectual way in our minds. Which of course he does – but not exclusively.

Martyn Lloyd-Jones comments: 'We must never forget that the Holy Spirit affects the whole person. You see, man is body, soul and spirit and you cannot divide these. Man reacts as a whole. And it is folly to expect that he can react in the realm of the spiritual without anything happening to the rest of him. . . Something is happening which is so powerful that the very physical frame is involved.'

Those who talk in a way that despises the emotions and the body, and elevates the mind/spirit, are often influenced by Greek dualism, which despised earthly reality and the material world.

The Bible warns us that our emotions and our bodies will be affected by the influence of sin. It also tells us that God loved his good creation (Gen 1) and that 'to the pure, everything is pure' (Titus). If the earth is the Lord's and everything in it, then God can use physical and emotional means, which he created, to draw us to him. In God's hands they can be pure.

Isn't some of what is happening at the moment a bit bizarre and unhelpfully sensational?

God doesn't always act in a quiet, hidden way. He had Ezekiel lie on his side for 390 days. He had David dance, with great abandon and to the disgust of his wife, before him. He had Hosea marry a prostitute. He caused a spiritual scandal which resulted in accusations of drunkenness on the Day of Pentecost.

His ways are not always our ways.

I went to a meeting where all this 'blessing' was supposed to be happening. I just didn't feel at peace. I got a real check in my spirit.

God speaks to us through our intuitions and our observations. It can be legitimate therefore to examine carefully what we have seen and heard and perhaps speak to those involved.

Not all who have the outward trappings of the current renewal will be handling it all wisely – or they may still be learning. I was in a meeting where I got no 'check' about the overall gathering and its integrity. I did however have a check about several individuals' behaviour.

There is a danger here. Ultra-subjective people, armed with a legalistic philosophy of ministry, will use their 'sense of peace' and their 'checks in my spirit' as a blunt instrument of prejudice, accusation and superficial spiritual judgement. They will see demons under every stone, and they won't leave many unturned. Beware those people whose entire identity is wrapped up in 'protecting the faithful'. They can sometimes destroy the faithful with division, accusation and false words of knowledge.

10

Wise Pastors

An anonymous pastor has reflected 'Am I missing the burning bush for trying to keep the lawn cut?' Combine this sentiment with Charles Haddon Spurgeon's assertion that 'revival is a season of glorious disorder' and you capture something of the dilemma of a pastor in the midst of a 'time of refreshing'.

Even stalwarts of revival stumble over the practical issues that arise. Jonathan Edwards, the New England revival leader quoted in Chapter 8, faced criticism because of the vigorous role being adopted by ordinary lay people. He subsequently curtailed the activity of lay people, and the fires of renewal were doused, until Whitefield visited the Northampton church several years later.

Other revival leaders and observers note that quenching the Spirit is not so much the problem, but rather having the discernment to weed out spiritual impostors.

William Gibson in *The Year of Grace* (Ambassador), a classic work on the 1859 Ulster revival, reflects on a minister greatly used during the revival who was faced with a prophet and a sleeper. These two arrived in a house meeting and one announced that the other would fall into a sleep and not awake for two hours. The minister and several others asked him what the point of the exercise was, suggesting it was bad mannered to just walk into a meeting and take over, and reminding him that prophetic ability did not necessarily indicate true faith, and they cited the case of Balaam (Num 22). The 'spiritual' showman and his friend were suitably distracted for over half an hour and the prophesied sleep did not materialise.

Pastors, leaders, elders and PCC members are seeking to grapple with this same tension. How does one discern that which is right from that which is distraction, or indeed false?

There is a recognition that learning from each other is vital. Several key churches have become focal points for pastoral gatherings. Queen's Road Baptist in Wimbledon, and the Covenant Ministries Leicester church, are two places where regular weekday meetings have been held for pastors and leaders. The Sunderland Christian Centre has gathered leaders from throughout the North East.

Much of the British expression of this time of refreshing is rooted in contact with, or respect for, the Vineyard movement. The result is that the Vineyard's regard for practical pastoral theology and pastoral frameworks is much in evidence.

From the start, churches such as the Toronto Vineyard and the Champaign Vineyard in Chicago have published guidance notes for their pastors and lay leaders. These have been widely circulated (and are reprinted in Patrick Dixon's excellent source book *Signs of Revival* – Kingsway) and British leaders such as Gerald Coates of Pioneer People and Bryn Jones of Covenant Ministries have published their own.

What are the issues that these documents address? They are vital indicators of the integrity of what many believe God is doing at present and a powerful antidote to accusations of unorthodoxy and irresponsibility.

The wise pastor is faced with several key questions:

● How can leaders conduct themselves with integrity at this time?

- When Paul speaks of meetings being conducted 'decently and in order' what exactly does he mean? How are we to respond to the disruption of normal patterns of worship and ministry?
- Refreshing and revival are nearly always accompanied by a resurgence of prophecy. How are leaders to ensure that this is weighed and acted upon, but not abused?
- How should we pray for people?
- What type of ministry is appropriate in a public meeting - should deliverance from demons be done in a private place?
- How can a leader encourage and facilitate renewal?

The role of the leader in renewal

For some leaders a move of the Holy Spirit will be deeply unsettling. Even if they are open-hearted they will necessarily be seeking to find a balance between control and anarchy.

Several key values for the leader emerge from the guidance notes widely circulated in the Vineyard churches, Pioneer, Covenant and Anglican churches in this country. What follows draws on their notes.

Integrity and humility

Rick Joyner, a prophetic figure active in the United States, has talked in *The Harvest* of a 'nameless, faceless' revival, whose leadership seem 'undistinguished and in some cases invisible. They will have no desire to build major ministries and will not covet fame or fortune.' This 'new breed, without fame or position, will direct some of the greatest events in history'. They will be 'selfless messengers of power' who will cause fear in the heart of Satan.

Bryn Jones, leader of the Covenant Ministries network of churches, in a letter to his leaders warns: 'Be careful not to seek to get maximum personal gain from what is a move of the Spirit.' He counsels humility and a willingness for the leader himself to be prayed for. He directs people back to Jesus. 'Be careful to maintain the focus on the true source of blessing – God Himself, and not to transfer people's faith to a man, a place or a method.'

These words of caution are vital. Rodney Howard-Browne is being used by God; Toronto has been a place where people have received renewal; laughing has been a symbol of release for many. God however is moving through other men, other places and in other ways.

Howard-Browne is wary of building a personality cult. In the late summer of 1994 he changed the name of his organisation to Revival Ministries International and dropped the RHBEA (Rodney Howard-Browne Evangelistic Association) identity.

Decently and in order

When speakers have to stop because so many are laughing or crying, or roaring, then the status quo can be judged to have been disturbed.

For some who have observed the meetings of recent months, the questions mount up. Why would the Holy Spirit, touching individual lives, interrupt the Holy Spirit who was inspiring the preacher?

For some the phrase 'decently and in order' simply refers to an orderly progress through the various aspects of the service, with physical manifestations apparent and not unwelcome as a result of the preaching or during specified times of ministry. For others, the phrase is much more loaded. They are wary of the shaking, the laughing and the unusual behaviour.

It may be tempting for the sympathetic church leader to 'let the meeting go', and attribute its direction to the Holy Spirit. Gerald Coates is wary: 'The elders in Corinth had a hands-off approach. What they were seeing was a mixture of the work of the Spirit, the work of the flesh and even the devil. As leaders we have to give an account of what we allow and encourage in our churches. God puts no premium on ignorance; whilst it's a time of refreshing, it is also a time when we as leaders must help the church understand what is happening.'

Rick Joyner is also cautious about unfettered spontaneity and speaks of congregations that claimed to be 'led entirely by the Holy Spirit, but were in fact being led more often by the immature and the rebellious'.

For some then 'decently and in order' means a responsible flexibility, a willingness to live between the opposite poles of detailed organisation and complete spontaneity.

Mona Johnian, author of *The Fresh Anointing*, and along with her husband Paul a leader of the Christian Teaching and Worship Center in Woburn near Boston, is happy to see their church's 'programmed meetings' disappear but is wary of chaos. 'Disorder occurs when no one is in charge, when no one knows what to do and when everyone is left to himself. What the Apostle Paul sought to correct at Corinth was each person expressing himself without regard to anyone else. In our services [my husband] Paul always remains visible. Together, he and I are continually bringing understanding about what is taking place.'

The Apostle Paul also makes it clear that spiritual expression may be subject to the person. No one *has* to do anything at any given moment. The spirits of the prophets are subject to the prophets (1 Cor 14:32). Each must, in fact, wait his or her turn so that all may benefit from what God is doing in their midst.

Some pastors and preachers are willing to abandon their plans in order to respond to the Holy Spirit touching lives. This is not easy for those whose culture has conditioned them to believe that God only moves as a response to preaching – preferably preaching centred on Calvary and Christ's work on the cross.

Any meaningful revival will exalt Jesus and the preaching of the cross, and the repentance that results will be a vital aspect. But to measure revival incidents simply by a 'preach-ing' criterion is to reduce revival to a formalised package and impugns the very sovereignty of God that many supremacy-of-preaching advocates would vigorously promote.

Paul, or Saul as he was on the road to Damascus, was not preached to – he was visited by God and confronted with a single sentence. 'Saul, Saul, why do you persecute me?' God has sparked revival and renewal many times with single sentences.

Joseph Jenkins was the pastor in a Methodist church in New Quay, Wales. He had prayed long and hard and preached diligently to promote a new godliness among his people. A young convert, Florrie Evans stood to witness at a youth meeting. Jenkins invited testimony and after a while the trembling Florrie stood up and simply said, 'I love the Lord Jesus with all my heart.' Eifor Evans, writing in *The Welsh Revival of 1904* comments: 'The effect was startling, and an overpowering sense of God's presence seemed to solemnise and yet excite the whole congregation.'

The spiritually renewed young people visited neighbour-ing churches to share the blessing so becoming one of the primary sparks of the 1904 revival.

The 1859 Ulster revival, which started in Connor, spread to Ahoghill, following the conversion of a young man at a cock-fight. His brother found him there and simply said, 'I have a message for you from the Lord Jesus.' John Weir writing in *Heaven Came Down* records: 'This went to his heart, he too felt the pangs of deep repentance; he too soon fled for refuge to the open arms of the crucified Redeemer.' The local minister, touched by this conversion, invited the Connor people to his church and revival spread.

The average preacher still struggles if his sermon is inter-rupted by anything other than tears of repentance or shouts of joy and affirmation.

The conduct of meetings at the Airport Vineyard is per-haps a helpful model. General Vineyard practice seems to be to believe that manifestations in a meeting might well be God, could possibly be the flesh, and on occasion might be the devil. Believing that rebuke is only used in extreme cases they will sometimes acknowledge an 'interruption' but nevertheless carry on. In this they may also be reflecting the attitude of Charles Wesley, whom John White records as having ignored unobtrusive 'performances' and removed noisy ones.

During my visit to the Airport Vineyard in August 1994, there were periodic interruptions from laughter and on one occasion a 'roaring lion'. The attitude of the pastor, John Arnott, was interesting. Some of the laughter was gentle and unobtrusive, but some was loud, long and infectious. Perhaps John was unwilling to make judgements about the laughter of strangers. He certainly did not feel constrained to stop, but simply asked for more volume on the microphone! Sometimes he would say something non-confrontational but firm such as, 'Let's listen closely to this now.' This had the effect of silencing those simply caught up in infectious laughter and often quietened the prime laughers too.

When a young Texan began roaring, John explained his belief that such things were a prophetic symbol of the anger of the Lion of Judah with sin and that the 'young lion' should eventually prophesy in English what God had placed in his heart.

As the roaring continued he reminded the congregation and the individual that the spirit of the prophet is subject to the prophet. Privately the Airport team encouraged the Texan church leaders to encourage the young man, but to help him bring maturity to how he expressed what he believed God was saying.

To a one-time-only visitor to a meeting, particularly a conservative Christian, these types of phenomena may be too much to bear. After witnessing them several times the interruptions may loom less large and a sense of confidence in the overall direction of the meetings can begin to emerge.

For those with a perfectionist mindset it will all be a little too messy. Allowances must be made for congregation members learning to respond appropriately to the Spirit, and for leaders learning to discern between the Spirit, the flesh and the devil. Judgements about a church's conduct on the basis of one meeting do a disservice to those involved. I was once 'pushed over' by a visiting preacher at a 1990 meeting. Outside observers might have assumed that such a practice was the norm. It most definitely wasn't. The international leaders of the church I belonged to remonstrated at length with the preacher involved.

Leaders must be ready to grasp the nettle of confrontation or reproof on occasion. The Airport Vineyard leader at one session I attended asked a member of the congregation to hold a 'word'. Vineyard pastor Mark Dupont, speaking at a July meeting in Kent, simply asked two women to be quiet. He and the other Airport leaders are wary of major deliverance (exorcism of demons) in public meetings.

Mark comments, 'As a rule, we don't want to do any deliverance during the ministry meetings in Toronto. We'll either bind the demonic spirit or take people out of the meeting. Private counselling can then take place.'

John Wimber, speaking to the Toronto congregation at a June 1994 conference, commented that it was necessary to keep teaching the Bible, and counsel those who need counsel even if normal routines are disrupted. 'There ought to be an ongoing routine. I believe in progressive, process-related sanctification. It's good to learn to pray, to read the Bible, to give, learn to attend church and serve others.'

Wimber also reflected on the 'decently and in order' passage in 1 Corinthians 14:40: 'It's dependent on how you read the text as to what meaning you derive. In my earlier conservative evangelical background, I would have read it in this way. Everything should be done in a *fitting* and *orderly* way. Fitting and orderly meant according to our traditions and our development.'

He suggests that the Lord challenged him that perhaps the passage should be read: '*Let everything be done*, in a fitting and orderly way. What's fitting and orderly to us may not be fitting and orderly to God.' He continued, 'I studied the Old Testament and discovered God is disorderly and unfitting (by our terms). I'd been taught that God is a gentleman, he'll never embarrass you. But what about a prophet called to be in the nude before his neighbours (Is 20). . . and all the others?' Wimber might easily have referred to Naaman, called to go and wash in a river, or Ezekiel, laid on his side for months on end.

It seems clear that key figures in this current time of refreshing are committed to keeping a careful eye out for the fleshly and the demonic, but they are happy to take risks with the unusual and with a disruption of their usual patterns.

Prophecy

Prophecy has played a part in the events leading up to this 'time of refreshing'. It has often had a significant role in revival, as a study of the life of Wesley and Jonathan Edwards demonstrates. Edwards did not feel much at ease with what we today might term the gifts of the Spirit and was not disposed to view the prophecies of his day as being of the 'same nature with the visions of the prophets, or Paul's rapture into Paradise'.

The re-emergence of prophecy as a significant part of the charismatic movement of the last thirty years has not been without its problems. Some have used 'prophecy' to justify immorality, others have had spurious 'words of knowledge' that have pinpointed non-existent and unverifiable sin or demonic influence in a person's life. Other prophetic figures have simply been misunderstood or have themselves been rebellious. If this current movement of God sparks a further release of prophetic gifting there are some who will be more alarmed than enthused.

Nonetheless in recent years a practical theology of the

prophetic has been developed among the various streams of the charismatic movement. Its proponents are in the vanguard of this current time of refreshing. Before we examine how they are helping to bring clarity and balance it may be as well to define what is meant by the terms 'prophecy' or 'prophetic'. There may be several shades of meaning.

- It may mean a helpful insight, word of Scripture, or song sung in a meeting or Christian gathering.
- It may mean a specific insight into a person's life. Just as Jesus knew the thoughts of his opponents or the sinful ways of the woman at the well, so the Holy Spirit may give people today a 'word of knowledge'.
- It may mean the application of the eternal word of God to today's world and culture so that rebuke or encouragement can be brought and strategy for the future discerned. Old Testament prophets such as Hosea, Micah and Amos, who exposed social injustice and reflected on God's standard, are examples. Evangelical social reformers such as Wilberforce (abolition of slavery) and Shaftesbury (ending of child labour and numerous other reforms) might well be considered prophetic figures.
- It can also mean specific foreknowledge about the future. The book of Acts records that the prophet Agabus predicted famine and persecution (Acts 11:28; 21:10).
- It can include dreams and visions and mental images or pictures.

It is also wide open to subjective emphasis of secondary details. Some who have dreams treat them as reality. A careful comparison of the 'caught up to heaven' stories of Morris Cerullo, Roberts Liardon and others reveals major discrepancies in the descriptions of Jesus, particularly in relation to his hair colour. . . .

In the light of this, Paul's admonition to the Thessalonians to 'test everything – hold on to the good' (1 Thess 5:21) is a sure foundation. Some equate questions with doubt.

Open-minded doubt is biblical. Closed-minded unbelief is what God abhors.

What then might constitute a responsible attitude towards the prophetic? The Airport Vineyard church has issued briefing notes, available to congregational members and visitors. This document represents a responsible stance and reflects the view of many of those who would identify themselves as being both evangelical in doctrine and charismatic in practice. They address several key concerns.

Prophecy in relation to Scripture. Rick Joyner, who along with Paul Cain and Bill Hamon is a leading figure in the prophetic movement, urges his readers in *The World Aflame* to hear from God today. He is clear however that: 'This is not to imply that this is for the establishing of new doctrines or to add to the canon of Scripture.'

He warns however: 'Many people become addicted to prophetic words. . . As we mature, we should need less guidance, not more. Having to hear from the Lord about every little decision can be a sign of immaturity, not maturity. Prophets are not meant to be gurus. Neither are the Scriptures meant to be used as a horoscope.'

The Airport Vineyard leaflet 'What to do when you receive prophetic words' is equally clear. 'There is however still the need to test all prophecies by the Spirit and the Word since "we prophesy in part" (1 Cor 13:9) i.e. no prophecy or prophet is infallible or equal in authority to the Bible.'

They further note that 'the Spirit of God will always agree with his previous revelation in the Bible' and urge the recipient to compare what they have heard to the Scripture.

Prophecy and accountability Given that contemporary prophets are not infallible, the recognition of this can help deflect an unreal idealism about prophecy. People can receive and weigh a prophecy and 'put it on the shelf' if it doesn't make immediate sense, or throw it out if it proves to be incorrect. The Airport pastoral team encourage people to ask questions about prophecy. Does it ring true and confirm what God has already spoken to you? Is it true? Are there factual statements in it that can be verified?

Those who share a prophetic word are usually on the church ministry team. The briefing note comments: 'You can be assured that those people, who from time to time minister in personal words to individuals, are under the authority and observation of the pastors who have the responsibility for the spiritual oversight of the church. You may be confident, therefore, of the relative maturity and of the trust which we have in them as loving, stable Christians and able ministers.'

The Airport Vineyard are wary of any kind of unhelpful prophecy. They warn against 'do or die' prophecies and note that prophecies which 'give specific dates, times, life partners, relationships, and exhortations to do something or not do something are reserved for the most mature and experienced' and even then all the criteria already mentioned apply, for even when the core of a prophetic word is correct, the time frames and details may be wrong.

Believing that bringing correction is a job for the wise and mature they counsel caution about 'corrective, judgmental or condemning prophecy, as it would not generally be from the Lord. Run it by one of the pastors if you have questions or doubts.'

Immature prophets receive short shrift. 'Sometimes people try to use their gifting to gain recognition in the body of Christ. We as a church are much more interested in character than in giftedness. Giftedness must flow out of wholeness, maturity and integrity. Sometimes "would be" prophets will do an end run around all the church safeguards, and give you a word in the parking lot, or some other private place. Avoid this like the plague.'

An openness to change

This is not always as difficult as it sounds. Many pastors testify to being close to burnout before their contact with this
wave of renewal. The idea that God would take hold of their
congregations and weed out backbiting, criticism, hard-
heartedness, and at the same time short-circuit the path to
maturity for some of the worst counselling problems, is not
unattractive, even if the price is change.

Gerald Coates comments: 'We must be willing to
embrace the work of God's Spirit even if it means changes to
our structures, programmes and agendas. The main key is
the entire leadership submitting themselves to the Holy
Spirit and being willing to receive prayer.'

Teamwork

The classic renewal pattern in many churches is built on a
model that presupposes that you don't spring change on a
congregation. Initial renewal often takes place among the
leadership team, then in small group meetings and then
finally in the main congregation.

While some churches have found themselves immersed
by God, as we discovered in earlier chapters, others have
sought out God's blessing and have had the opportunity to
discover a time of refreshing at a slower pace.

Given the contentious nature of much of the phenomena
it's helpful to ensure that those leading meetings, or praying
with others, share the vision of the church, support the leadership and are open to the activity of the Holy Spirit.

When a church becomes involved in ministry to a wider
circle of Christians, or simply to larger numbers, other team-
work issues come to the fore.

In order to guard the integrity of what is happening some
churches request that only the designated ministry team,
usually with badges, pray for people. This helps guard
against freelance extremists or even enemies of renewal

praying for people and promoting unhelpful doctrines or
insights, particularly with respect to extreme doctrines of
demonic deliverance or a non-accountable prophetic ministry.

In order to facilitate growth and understanding some
churches encourage non-ministry-team people to stand
alongside ministry team members and even participate in the
prayer. The team member provides accountability and wisdom as appropriate.

Focus on Christ and the fruits of refreshing

Beware, counsels Bryn Jones, of concentrating on a man, a
method or a place. David Pytches, no personal stranger to
manifestations such as roaring like a lion, discourages a
'striving to manifest strange and often amusing phenomena'.

Leadership should encourage those who testify to concentrate on the interior change that God has brought about as
a result of their meeting with him.

Given the fact that some respond to ministry because in
the heightened atmosphere of a meeting laughter or falling is
infectious, the leader will also want to avoid a 'ministry of
manifestations' where a great deal happens physically but no
substantial engagement has taken place.

Following John Arnott around the Toronto Vineyard one
discovers a variety of needs being met and transactions with
God taking place. Some need physical healing, others emotional healing. Some have sin to confess, others joy to
express.

At a meeting in my own home church in Eastbourne, one
couple in their forties spoke of their initial fear, how God
swept over them and the subsequent sense that a cloud of
depression over their lives had evaporated.

Lois Gott, part of the leadership team at the Sunderland
Christian Centre, appeared at the close of their Saturday meet-
ing on 10th September, with mascara all over her white jacket.
She had counselled several girls and women. One had spoken

of the need to stop living a double life, the others about giving up smoking. They hadn't merely had an experience, they were being challenged at the ethical core of their lives.

This contrasts with a church where the early part of the meeting was marked by a 'demonstration of God's power' as the leader systematically pushed people over. Quite what was happening to them in terms of an encounter with God is open to conjecture.

A concentration on the physical takes people's focus away from Jesus and the fruit he desires, but we can't ignore the sheer physical impact of some people's meetings with God. We should regard it however as secondary to the real business of inner transformation.

Bringing balance

It doesn't seem unreasonable that God might interrupt our plans and dispense with the sermon at a meeting, should he choose to. He might even disrupt us more than once. But is it likely that we will go ten weeks without a sermon, as one church is reputed to have done?

No, not likely, according to even the most enthusiastic supporters of freedom and openness. Martyn Relf, pastor of the Living Stones church in Eastbourne, unknowingly echoed the sentiments of John Wimber when he reminded the congregation that in the midst of blessing, the nitty, gritty of church life would continue. We'll still be preaching the word and doing all the other things that build up the church.

Bryn Jones is equally emphatic: 'We must continue our commitment to the word and the Spirit and not find ourselves caught in the trap of word or Spirit, where Christians lurch from side to side.'

Introspection is out

Given the self-centred nature of our society it would be easy for us to get caught up in the 'pursuit of perpetual excitement' that sometimes symbolises extreme groups and selfish individuals. While God desires to sort us out, the healing process for many involves a turning outwards, a decision to serve God rather than merely seek emotional and spiritual perfection for oneself.

Bryn Jones, writing for the Covenant Ministries Network, reflects: 'The purpose of a refreshing is to contribute to the fulfilling of the ultimate objectives of God's purpose.' Gerald Coates is equally outward looking: 'We want to see people ultimately look to those outside the Christian community. Otherwise self-indulgence will take root. . . and eventually we will dry up.'

Instruct and explain

Ken Gott, pastor of the Sunderland Christian Centre, handed me the microphone and disappeared into the 400-strong congregation to pray for men who had responded to a call for prayer. As he and the women of the church prayed, men fell to the ground, some weeping, others apparently in a trance-like state.

The previous night there had been similar scenes as I started to preach after several had received prayer. I was coping with the noise, but the 200 or so attending that church for the first time were curious. I had persevered, not least because those stricken shouted their agreement with my more emphatic points!

On the Sunday morning I did what I should have done the previous night. I explained to the congregation what was happening to various individuals.

Explaining and interpreting has a dual function. It clarifies issues for people and helps them understand. Relating some of the experiences to Scripture helps make it clear that we are not 'awash in a sea of subjectivity'. It signals that the meeting is still proceeding and, while it is not being rigidly controlled, it nevertheless still has direction and purpose. Explanation will often satisfy curiosity and help the whole congregation concentrate once more on the continuing flow of the meeting.

Rest!

Reading the history of revival, particularly those intense periods when meetings took place nightly in New England and in Ulster in 1859, one often comes across pastors close to exhaustion as they helped at meetings and visited the homes of those still physically stricken after their encounter with God and needing further prayer. Is their workload being repeated?

While some churches have become 'refreshment centres' and are meeting nightly, others have simply added another midweek meeting and/or extra Sunday meeting.

Even in the 'refreshment centre' churches such as Sunderland Christian Centre or the Airport Vineyard, an average of 10-30% of the home congregation are out every night. Most home congregation people attend more than once a week, but few come every night.

It's important for everyone to be aware of the necd for rest and balance. Gerald Coates cautions, 'Continually giving out, without receiving, can lead to exhaustion and burnout. Take time to receive, rest, read Scripture and do "normal" things. God wants us to be around for the long haul, not a short sprint.'

11

Wading in the Water

A common word picture currently in use is drawn from Ezekiel 47, where a river of life-giving water flows out from the temple and nourishes the land, providing fruit for food and leaves for healing. The prophet had originally waded in the water at ankle depth, but he eventually reached a point where the river was so deep that he could have swum in it.

The renewed church around the world would appear to be in the shallows, their ankles wet, but anticipating that they will soon be swimming in a torrent of Holy Spirit blessing, that will cause everything it touches to live.

Where will the Lord take us next? The hope is for a revival that will wash over the unchurched and the nominal and deeply touch the core values of this nation and many others. The crossover point will be when significant numbers of non-Christians profess faith in Christ. The historical impact of such revival is well documented.

Jerry Steingarden reminds his Hamilton Vineyard congregation of the impact of revival on Wales in a special briefing paper.

Crime dropped off to the point where many courtrooms and jails were empty. Some policemen formed singing quartets and sang in the revival meetings because there was so little to do while they were on duty.

Horses in the coal mines were accustomed to obeying commands that involved yelling and cursing. When the vast majority of miners were converted, the horses were confused with commands that were humane and wholesome, and needed retraining.

Duncan Campbell, ministering during the Hebridean revival of 1949, left one meeting only to discover 600 people outside. One hundred were from the nearby dance hall, the others had in many instances got up out of bed, dressed and come to church, compelled by the Holy Spirit. He had to leave them at 4.00 am to minister to 400 gathered at the police station. As he travelled he came across people along the road crying out to God for mercy. Krupp, writing in *The Church Triumphant*, notes that an estimated 75% of the converts came to faith in Jesus in circumstances that did not involve a church building!

Similar patterns were witnessed in the 1859 revival in Ulster. John Weir, reflecting on the revival in Ballymena in *Heaven Came Down*, records: 'Strong crying, tears and prayers were heard in the streets. . . It was found that those once the most careless and wicked, and worldly, now crowded the different places of worship. In some streets, four or five crowds of people, in houses and before the open doors and open windows, engaged in prayer and praise.'

Part of the effect of the Ulster revival, noted by Ian Paisley in *The Fifty-Nine Revival* was the sale of one brewery and the closing down of another. One pastor, the Revd Theophilus Campbell, noted that eight local prostitutes in one area had given up their trade. The Revd J. Baillie also noted that a former brothel was now used for prayer meetings. These were but the tip of the reformation iceberg, with a decline in drunkenness, sectarian conflict between Catholics and Protestants, and violence.

The whole moral tenor of Wales, Ireland and the Hebrides was changed by this touch of God. Should we desire any less?

The social fabric of countries affected by Western culture

is being destroyed. The cumulative effects of rebellion against God's wisdom unleash emotions and forces that tear apart families and institutions. Premarital or extra-marital sex reflects the corruption of the sexual urge away from God's intention for it within the covenant relationship of marriage. God's good gift becomes an idol. The fruit of this idolatry is children who are inadequately parented, families where truth is destroyed by infidelity, and all kinds of sexual violence.

This is but a snapshot of the idolatrous nature of our society. Some worship power and seek it through the occult. For some 'their god is their stomach' and a life characterised by materialistic desires and over-indulgence is the norm.

In an essentially self-centred society reformational change must percolate up – as a fruit of personal moral change – as well as down, through a society where a prophetic stand is taken against economic injustice, pornography, abortion, racism and all that assaults the dignity of human beings made in the image of God.

Can we believe that God will release this kind of revival in our time? What might hinder him? It may be helpful to look at the first Great Awakening of the 1740s and aspects of the Welsh revival for guidance as to what can quench the flow of the Spirit.

Unhelpful confrontation

Whitefield and Davenport, active in the first Great Awakening, did not always handle their anger with the reproach of their critics too well. They denounced some in the most intemperate terms, telling them to their faces that they were not fit to be in charge of a church.

As the church swims in the river, there are going to be some who behave unhelpfully. The lifeguards on the bank will then issue stern warnings about proper behaviour in the water. For those swimming carefully it can be more than a little vexing. Exaggeration, selective evidence, intolerance, heresy masquerading as truth, snap judgements, guilt by association, will carry some beyond proper Berean-style healthy scepticism and into outright opposition.

How is the revived believer to respond? A sense of grief over the sheer destructiveness of a hasty judgement or ill-considered dismissal can easily turn into anger and railing. Jonathan Edwards warned friends of revival to avoid an 'angry zeal' and a judgemental attitude towards those who did not share the revivalist stance.

Gerald Coates, in a letter to the Pioneer network of churches, counsels people to avoid 'reactionary, cynical, dismissive or superior attitudes. Remain calm, rational and reasonable. Learn to disagree without being disagreeable.' If we are to avoid the accusation that we lack the fruit of genuine Holy Spirit renewal, we will need to heed that word.

If we don't, God will remove his hand of blessing. He doesn't bless sectarianism.

'Mighty man' syndrome

Jonathan Edwards was severely censured by his fellow clergymen for letting lay people take a prominent role. There was to be little room for people to learn from their mistakes, and the revival began to wane.

While God still uses sold-out individuals to further his purposes, the experiences of Evan Roberts in the Welsh revival, where enthusiasm waned following his retirement from Wales in 1907, should suggest that God desires, as he did in the 1857-59 worldwide revival, to use the whole church. Jesus didn't just raise up Peter to evangelise the Jewish nation. He had twelve disciples and a band of seventy-two whom he also sent out. His 'inner circle' would seem to have been 500 strong, if the number to whom he appeared after his resurrection is any measure.

Notwithstanding the various strands of evangelical and

charismatic life from which this time of refreshing has grown, the strong emphasis of the Vineyard movement on lay training is important.

They emphasise that God looks at the heart, and desires a growing holiness in his servants. But while that holiness is maturing God will still use people to bless others and to do miracles. This contrasts with the philosophy often inherent in some Pentecostal/charismatic literature which seems to suggest that mighty miracle workers are a special breed, extremely devout, holy, totally surrendered and soaked in the word. Not that those things are wrong – they should be the goal of us all – but a truly effective church doesn't need a few superpreachers pulling huge audiences. It needs mighty people planting a myriad of churches.

The Vineyard model is not unique to them, but it has been important that one of their churches has been a modelling church in the midst of renewal. It encourages the idea that God will use people generally, not just extraordinary individuals.

Spiritual anarchy

The ability to walk a tightrope would be an excellent skill for those involved in renewal and revival. A leader of a large mission group – who would not make big decisions without a 'word from the Lord' – once told me of his efforts to help the group find a balance between spiritual revelation and biblical principles, the latter requiring no special permission from God.

Unlike the circus act, there is no spiritual safety net. If you're not balanced, you crash to the ground.

Unfettered, spontaneous meetings can lead to spiritual aimlessness, a directionless drift into the 'pursuit of perpetual excitement', with the next big spiritual breakthrough always just around the corner.

George Jeffreys, pioneer of the Elim movement, writing

in 1933, encouraged people to go beyond manifestations to lasting fruit. He wrote:

> Revival has broken out - the Spirit descends, the miraculous gifts are in evidence, and everything is on the move. Then, to the consternation of wise heads, the hands are taken off the proper controls, and the power and gifts are allowed to run uncontrolled. The New Testament pattern of church equilibrium is upset, and it is not long before undue emotionalism, accompanied by excessive psychic forces, comes aboard, with the result that the church in due time is split into pieces. . . The genuineness of the dynamic cannot be questioned, for there was nothing wrong with it. The trouble was caused by not acknowledging the need of control so clearly revealed by the Scriptures. Those in charge discovered too late that there was no real bondage in scriptural control, and no real liberty in uncontrolled power.

The greatest danger in terms of spiritual anarchy is the possible rise of a sectarian spirit among those involved in renewal, whereby they vigorously denounce those who oppose them or who do not share similar experiences or patterns. Humility, unity and the kind of principled tolerance which does not fudge over differences, but seeks to accentuate areas of common agreement, are all vital if the river of God is to flood our churches and society.

'Here is love, vast as the ocean'

If our hearts are right and we do not hinder and quench the Spirit of God, heaven might well come down, and glory will fill our souls.

The 1859 Ulster revival is perhaps the most helpful model that we have. If the 1859 experience and the current time of refreshing are examined within a framework which embraces the five marks of revival identified by J. I. Packer, the respected evangelical theologian, a positive picture emerges.

An awareness of God's presence

The presence of God, witnessed to by many at this time, is something that is perceived both objectively and subjectively. Sick people are healed, broken relationships are restored. Fresh understandings of God, Jesus and the Holy Spirit are both observed in the Scripture and discovered in one's own subjective experience through dreams and visions.

Some have literally felt the presence of God resting on them 'like a warm blanket', or a weight.

As you have worked through this book you will have read many testimonies of people's lives utterly transformed by a fresh encounter with the Holy Spirit. That which is mysterious, intangible and beyond our imagination to comprehend, has in some way been made manifest. Enticed by this glimpse of heaven's power, might we ask God for what Tom Shaw has described as a 'prayer burden that never slackened until God rent the heavens and mountains of sin and evil flowed down at his presence' (*Heaven Came Down: The 1859 Revival* – Ambassador).

If we believe our Bibles we must believe it can happen again – that prevailing prayer will flow from the hearts of people who have a passion for Jesus. They will be hungry to know more about him, to pursue friendship with him through prayer, and be like him in every way.

They will be a holistic people. Their hearts will be in love with God, their minds will seek his wisdom and they will be active in his service in every aspect of their life, from work to family to creativity to church, and all points in between.

God is everywhere, but sometimes he is more apparent, his activities more visible – particularly when you allow his Holy Spirit to work through you. That is why God has been refreshing his tired, battle-worn, sin-battered people: so his presence can be more apparent; so that an ocean of love can flow out over our pain-wracked, rebellious, confused society.

Eat the word

Packer speaks of revival sparking a greater responsiveness to the word. A kind of fierce joy seized me when I read this. Preparing a sermon on 'Imagine what a tender-hearted generation could do' after my return from Toronto, I literally leapt to my feet when I read, 'I run in the paths of your commands because my heart is free' (Ps 119:32). Free from sin's shackles and destruction, I can gladly accept the confines of the path of God's wisdom.

A greater responsiveness to God's word will flow in direct proportion to the extent to which we help people grasp the wisdom of God. The Scripture tells us that God says, 'When your heart is wise, my heart is glad' (Prov 23:15). Legalism destroys, as does the preaching of God's justice to the detriment of an equal emphasis on his grace. But words, verses and passages can come alive afresh as they are read or expanded. Churches swept by the Spirit neglect the Scriptures at their peril. The Sunderland Christian Centre have a sermon at the majority of their meetings, but they have also designated Thursday night a special Bible study night. Over 500 are attending at the time of writing.

Preachers who are passionate for Jesus and in love with his wisdom can confront congregations with their need of forgiveness and can pour that wisdom into the hearts and minds of the people.

The Bible is the story of salvation, laced with practical wisdom. It is rich food if we will eat it. Hiding it in our hearts, so that it can instinctively be on our minds and on our lips, allows the Holy Spirit to speak to us and through us. The current emphasis on biblical meditation is a spiritual straw in the wind. The Ulster church, revived in 1859, had laid foundations as we shall see in a moment. A hunger for wisdom and an immersion in the word are but two ways God is preparing a church fit to disciple the unchurched and nominal who will flock to the sound of his name in the coming years.

Sensitivity to sin

Keri Jones, a leading figure in the Covenant Ministries network, writing in the summer 1994 edition of *Covenant* said, 'The Lord is re-emphasising that his word is to be obeyed. Through obedience we are finding that his ways are pleasant and his paths are peaceful.'

Gerald Coates told *The Daily Telegraph*, 'I have never had so many confessions of sin, letters of apology and acts of reconciliation.'

People freshly sensitive to God and alive to his wisdom begin to feel very uncomfortable about sin. They know its destructiveness, the trust it betrays, the bitterness it breeds, the emotional and physical violence it unleashes. If our relationship with the law-giver is good, his values are reflected in our other relationships. His commands are not arbitrary but promote a positive pattern of living. People will choose either to worship the Father of wisdom or idolise their own desires.

Kevin Prosch, the songwriter whose songs feature heavily at the Toronto Vineyard, in a song which brought me to tears the first time I heard it, writes, 'Break our hearts with the things that break yours. . . Help us to weep as Jesus wept, a fountain of tears for the broken and lost. . . who ever heard of an army of God, who conquered the earth by weeping, mourning and brokenness?' ('Break our hearts' – Mercy Publishing.)

You might have heard that this is a laughing revival. It is, and many who laugh are receiving in joy what they have sown in tears over the years. But ultimately, this is a weeping revival. Not a sad revival, for liberation brings joy, but a weeping revival because only a desperate, sick-of-sin people will have the persistence and passion to wait on God for the empowerment needed for revival evangelism.

It was the same in 1859. The people of Ulster turned in an astonishing way from sin. As we have already noted, sectarian violence decreased, brothels closed down, drunkenness all but disappeared, families were restored, relationships reconciled.

It must happen to us. One woman, making her way through the crowd at a large meeting recently, stumbled and almost fell, and was caught by someone she had been in conflict with for over five years. They wept together, their friendship was restored, and they are now ministering together in their local church.

May the Lord help us to hate sin, not because of false pride or a desire for reputation, but because our hearts are full of the love of the Father and we cannot stand to see the dignity of people made in the image of God destroyed or condemned by lies, broken promises and rebellion.

A heart for community

The prime movers in the 1859 Ulster revival were not well-known preachers, but local ministers. Their focus was not on a short-term crusade visit but on the long-term spiritual health of their neighbourhoods.

Evangelicals, driven by their own sectarian divides, have spent much of the last forty years seeking to be the one, true, holy, pure, doctrinally correct witness in their town. The illusion of growth, as the sectarian groups swapped congregation members, sustained them. But it is fading now.

The advent of a church-planting philosophy, where a church for a neighbourhood is envisaged, is beginning to undermine 'one-true-church' elitism. Terry Virgo, leader of the New Frontiers network, told his churches gathering for the 1994 Stoneleigh Bible week, 'His strategy of church planting is our priority. As we gather to worship God, be instructed and be empowered by the Holy Spirit, we shall be freshly commissioned for this great task.'

In a town like Eastbourne, where I am based, many of the evangelical churches of whatever kind concentrate their outreach on their neighbourhood. People still seek out churches that reflect their tastes, but evangelistic effort is oriented towards long-term friendship-building in the local community. This facilitates the rise of a 'mighty people' philosophy not an exclusive 'mighty man' evangelist model. Evangelism is the work of the whole church and evangelism is rooted in life, and not merely in statements of religious faith.

As we noted earlier in respect to the 1859 revival in Ballymena, many of the most profound scenes of revival took place in homes. Sandy Millar, Vicar of Holy Trinity Brompton, is emphatic that this will be an emphasis once again. He emphasises the ministry of the pastorate or home group as the place where the Christian life is 'lived out in affirmation of relationships and active response to God's world'. Writing in *HTB In Focus* he comments, 'It is there that the effects of ministry will be seen and it is through the ministering home group that the world will be touched.'

On 14th August he told his readers, 'Churches are growing faster where the vision for growth through homegroups has been restored... concentrating their attention on the home as the place for drawing neighbours in, mothers and toddlers, wives' groups, evening adult groups and every other sort of activity that is inspired by the Spirit of God as a means of a family being the Body of Christ in that locality.'

Sandy notes that Paul wrote to Priscilla and Aquila, Archippus and Nympha in various of his letters and greeted the church that met in their home. He cites the responsibility of families for sections of the wall when Nehemiah was helping rebuild Jerusalem, and concludes that we need to 're-think the possibilities of the use of our homes'. All this builds to his affirmation of lay people. 'If the purposes of God are going to be fulfilled in these days it will be because the lay people have understood the importance of their taking a lead and getting on with the job. The future is in your hands. The role of the clergy is to encourage and lead, but the task is the congregation's.'

The Holy Spirit flows where he will, but he also chooses to flow through us. An insular, non-neighbourhood church whose members have no social contact with the unchurched will not have the natural channels of influence that caused revival to spread in the close-knit communities of the Ulster countryside and Welsh valleys. In our lonely, city communities only an active Christian commitment to community involvement will enable us to be living demonstrations of the Holy Spirit at work.

If we then take seriously Sandy Millar's empowering of the laity, we will be reflecting another pattern prevalent in the 1859 Ulster revival. The Revd John Moore, a minister in Connor, had broken down his two large Sunday schools into thirteen smaller ones. He 'bestowed great labour' on the training of teachers. Four of the young men in the parish met regularly for prayer, and the minister told his congregation what 'the Lord was doing for his vineyard in America'.

Some of the most profound revival meetings were addressed by lay people. On Monday 14th March 1859 a crowd of 3,000 lingered after an official service had closed in Ahoghill. John Weir, writing in *Heaven Came Down* (Ambassador) records, 'A young convert addressed them and under the mighty influence of his appeals many fell down in the muddy streets and amid chilling rain, and poured forth earnest cries and prayers.' Weir notes that for several months prior to this someone in almost every one of the 700-plus households in the district had prayed and waited 'for the Holy Spirit'.

The sheer volume of prayer meetings and home meetings in 1859 made it imperative that the ministers delegated some work to lay people. In the white-hot spiritual climate of the June 1859 revival in Ballymena, several young men 'gave up almost their entire time, day and night, during the first week to minister to the religious instruction, and the physical and spiritual comfort of the poor stricken sufferers'.

God has been preparing us for such a time as this, just as he prepared through training and patient work those who would reap the 1859 harvest. Small groups, church planting and every-member ministry have been part of a reclaimed biblical and evangelistic heritage – God's provision for the time when the trickle of glory becomes a stream and then a flood.

Fruitfulness in testimony

We have already noted the importance of prayer as a prelude to revival. Duncan Campbell, the pivotal preacher in the 1949 Hebridean revival, was adamant about the importance of prayer. A number of men and two elderly women 'entered into a solemn covenant that they would not rest or cease from prayer until he made "Jerusalem" a praise on the island [of Lewis]'. The men would pray through the night and the two elderly sisters prayed for three nights every week. They were 'pleading one promise: "I will pour water upon him that is thirsty, and floods upon the dry ground."'

Their prayer was heard, as were the prayers of another group of villagers. Faced with great indifference another group of villagers met all night for prayer in a farmhouse. Duncan Campbell, writing in *The Price and Power of Revival* (Faith Mission), records that it was not an easy time. Around midnight he asked one young man to pray. The lad cried out, 'Lord, you made a promise, are you going to fulfil it?. . . I tell thee now that I am thirsty, oh, I am thirsty for a manifestation of thy right hand. Lord, before I sit down, I want to tell you that your honour is at stake.'

The house shook like a leaf, the dishes rattled. One elder said to Campbell, 'Mr Campbell, an earth tremor.' Campbell left the house to find men and women arriving at the church, some on their faces in distress of soul.

The church of the nineties is seeing unprecedented activity in respect of the promotion of prayer. The worldwide

March for Jesus on June 25th 1994 saw at least twelve million people unite for prayer. As many as thirty million had
prayed throughout October 1993 for spiritual breakthroughs
in the 10/40 window, the least evangelised area of the world
and home of most of the world's Buddhists, Muslims and
Hindus.

This global activity is matched by significant local
growth. The Argentinian Pentecostal community has
embarked on an aggressive prayer evangelism strategy that
has seen the church in the city of Resistancia grow first
102%, then a further 400% in the next two years, while the
seventy churches increased to an estimated 200. A significant part of the strategy was 600 neighbourhood prayer cells,
one for every hundred homes.

The British church is currently embracing several prayer
initiatives, with Prayer for Every Home (PFEH) seeking to
ensure that every home in the nation has been prayed for.
Perhaps a now dormant scheme, once promoted by the
Evangelical Alliance and known as 'A Light in Every Street'
should be resurrected.

Not only will prayer release God's blessing – so will
unity. In Christian communities around the world, pastors
are gathering to pray. They are then gathering in each other's
churches to ask God to give success to other pastors'
churches.

The 1859 revival was marked by meetings for united
prayer, including one that so filled the Belfast Botanic Gar-
dens that separate meetings sprang up for people who
couldn't hear the speaker in the main meeting. A day is coming when British believers will fill parks and stadia to worship and pray. The Spirit of God will fall at large open-air
gatherings and unbelievers will come to faith. The prayer of
a united church will be instrumental in the release of an outpouring of God's glory. Pastors will gather in each other's
churches to ask God to bless that congregation. Christians
will gather in their lunch hours in churches near to business

and industrial areas and ask God to pour out his 'latter rain'.

The intercessory prayer that will sweep the nation will be rooted in a Holy-Spirit-sparked compassion for the lost and rebellious. People who could hardly bear to pray will be spending nights in prayer. The curse of self-centred Christianity will be broken in many lives as people allow themselves to be transformed in their patterns of thinking by a new passion for Jesus, not a passion for self-fulfilment.

A church desperate for revival, calling out to God, will find a world that is more ready to listen than at any time this century. The enlightenment worldview, which placed the rational mind on an idolatrous pedestal, having an optimistic view of human nature, has been tried and found wanting. A litany of disaster trails in its wake: nuclear weaponry, pollution, genocide from both communist and fascist regimes, horrific slaughter in Yugoslavia, sadistic violence glorified at the heart of Western culture by the film industry.

A people who have lost faith in the global solutions turn inwards and embrace folk religion such as horoscopes or alternative medicine, and spiritualists such as Doris Stokes begin to rise again.

Children brought up on a TV diet of occult and Eastern mystical culture are already absorbing a supernatural worldview at odds with the materialistic one that for so long dominated Western culture. In their teenage years many edge closer to explicit spirituality through their interest in music and the spiritualities of occult-influenced heavy rock bands and some pagan-influenced dance/house/rave bands. Computer game culture, particularly adventure-role-play games, further feed the spiritual fire. Our culture is therefore more susceptible to and less sceptical about the supernatural than ever before.

It is also less reticent about personal vulnerability. Shows such as *Kilroy Silk*, *The Time The Place*, *Oprah* and *Donahue*, all screened on prime time television, have provoked a humanistic culture of 'confession' and public 'witness'

Add to this heady mix the growing prevalence of humanis-
tic/mystical evangelists and you have a climate where the
supernatural, the personal and the proclamatory appear to be
the norm. What do we mean by humanistic evangelists? The
growth of satellite and cable TV in Europe will allow for the
rise of the 'info-mercial' – a mix of testimonies, preaching
and an invitation to make a decision. These are not being
produced by Christians but by people promoting weight-loss
programmes, personal growth seminars and a variety of spiritualities. All promise a form of salvation.

All of these – folk religion, folk confession and fake
church – present both an opportunity and a challenge. The
church cannot remain silent while the humanistic evangelists steal our prophetic thunder by their addressing the dis-
tortion and sin in society. Their idolatrous solutions, calling
on 'the power within' or whatever, take needy people into
deception and further self-centredness.

So how can the church address this spiritual hunger?

A lifestyle of witness will be the appropriate response.
This will often involve us in understanding evangelism as an
essentially non-religious activity. For many of us, evangelism will be our deeds – our approach to work, our relationships with neighbours and unchurched friends, our involvement in social compassion, our integration into local
community activities. When the deeds have spoken, then the
bold (but polite) words can follow.

For many of us there needs to be a fresh understanding of
the nature of conversion. Most people undergo a process that
brings them to the point where they ask God to forgive their
rebellion and rule in their lives. Spectacular conversions are
the exception, not the norm. Like Paul on Mars Hill we must
seek to help people who have little or no concept of God to
begin to understand. Paul spoke of Greek poets and their
worship of an unknown God. He spoke in the cultural terms
of his day.

Another lesson from the book of Acts concerns Peter

(Acts 2). Confident that his hearers did have some perception of God, and an expectation of the Messiah, he came straight to the point. He spoke the truth directly at the right time. Together with his fellow disciples he expressed that truth in the 'mother tongue' of his listeners. Given their roots most would have understood Hebrew or Aramaic, but they heard the gospel in the everyday languages used in the places where they had settled.

We too must speak the mother tongues of our culture, expressing timeless, unchanging truth in preaching and musical styles, metaphors and pictures that reflect the diversity of our culture.

The church in revival will be diverse and multifaceted. Some will be quiet and meditative, others exuberant and expressing their worship through the music of the streets.

Social impact

Clive Calver, General Director of the Evangelical Alliance, speaking at Holy Trinity Brompton's July church holiday, reflected, 'I believe that God starts with us. But we don't want it to finish here, do we? I like laughing, but I'd like our world to laugh too.'

Clive is not simply referring to the possibility that some might come to know the joy of salvation, but the possibility that society might begin to be transformed or changed through Christian witness and institutions.

Brian Edwards, writing in *Revival* (Evangelical Press) reflects on the eighteenth- and nineteenth-century revivals in England and concludes, 'Revival gave the nation a social conscience and produced the men and women who campaigned for the abolition of slavery, and brought the women and children up from the mines, and boys down from the chimneys: revival contributed also to a greater concern for prisoners and the insane, a reduction in the hours of work and a care for the living conditions of the poor.'

Evangelicalism in the United Kingdom already has several institutions that have a wide social vision. These include Care Trust; Tear Fund, a relief and development agency; and Christmas Cracker, a youth project which has raised over £3 million in five years for Third-World relief.

The Shaftesbury Society is active in compassion, particularly for the disabled. The Jubilee Centre promotes a variety of political initiatives which aim to encourage the government of the day to hold the stable family as the core of its social policy. The Jubilee Campaign, with its roots in *Buzz* – the evangelical magazine of the seventies and eighties – is one of the leading human rights and religious liberty agencies in the world, with the support of over eighty members of Parliament.

At a local level many churches have involved themselves in community action. The South East London PECAN project has brought together a coalition of churches to help run Job Clubs. These clubs equip those who attend with the practical and communication skills that will help people re-enter the work force. A report in *The Independent* newspaper highlighted the significantly better results they achieved than central and local government-run schemes.

All of the above is but the tip of the social compassion iceberg. Jesus' parable of the sheep and goats in Matthew 25, which exhorts us to feed the poor and clothe the naked, combines with the warnings of Amos, Hosea and Micah against those who would sell the poor for a pair of sandals, to remind us that a revived church will also seek justice.

The framework is already built. A revived church should release resources and people to proclaim a Christian vision of justice and social compassion.

Clive Calver's words to the people gathered at Focus '94 perhaps sum up this moment in our history when we sense a turning point has been reached.

This is just a beginning – and as God gets surrendered lives, he wants to take us out to make a difference.

It's a call to repentance. It's a call to follow Jesus. It's a call to surrender ourselves. When we do that we'll stop waiting for God and find that God's waiting for us. And when he's found us I believe he's going to use us to change this nation in a way that we haven't seen since Wesley and Whitefield.

* * *

Be glad, O people of Zion,
rejoice in the Lord your God,
for he has given you the autumn rains in righteousness.
He sends you abundant showers,
both autumn and spring rains, as before.
The threshing-floors will be filled with grain;
the vats will overflow with new wine and oil.
I will repay you for the years the locusts have eaten. . .
and you will praise the name of the Lord your God,
who has worked wonders for you.

(Joel 2:23-26)

Dave Roberts is the editor of *Alpha*, Britain's leading evangelical monthly magazine. He is also the Publishing and Development Director for Elm House Christian Communications and as such is involved in the ministry of *Youthwork*, *Children's Ministry* and *Parentwise* magazines. He is also involved in youth leader training and a major Third-World charity.

If you have stories of how God has moved in renewal and revival in recent months, he would be pleased to hear from you. Dave is also available to speak.

Information and enquiries should be addressed to:

Dave Roberts
Box No 777
37 Elm Road
New Malden
Surrey
KT3 3HB
081 942 9761 or
0860 119427

Bibliography

Bickle, Mike. *Passion for Jesus*. Kingsway: Eastbourne, 1994.

Campbell, Duncan. *The Price and Power of Revival*. Faith Mission: Edinburgh.

Carson, John T. *God's River in Spate*. Presbyterian Church in Ireland: Belfast, 1958.

Chevreau, Guy. *Catch the Fire*. HarperCollins: London, 1994.
 Daniel Rowland. Banner of Truth: Edinburgh, 1985.

Deere, Jack. *Surprised by the Power of the Spirit*. Kingsway: Eastbourne, 1994.

Dixon, Patrick. *Signs of Revival*. Kingsway: Eastbourne, 1994.

Edwards, Jonathan. *On Revival*. Banner of Truth: Edinburgh, 1984, 1987, 1991.

Egerton, Gilbert. *Flame of God*. Ambassador: Belfast, 1987.

Evans, Eifion. *The Welsh Revival of 1904*. Evangelical Press of Wales, 1969.

Gibson, Wilson. *The Year of Grace*. Ambassador: Belfast, 1860, 1989.

Howard-Browne, Rodney. *The Touch of God*. Revival Ministries International: Louiseville, 1992.
 The Coming Revival. Revival Ministries International: Louiseville, 1990.

Jones, Brynmor Pierce. *The King's Champions*. Christian Literature Press: Cwmbran, 1968, 1986.

Joyner, Rick, *The World Aflame*. Morningstar: Charlotte 1993.
 The Harvest. Morningstar: Charlotte, 1989, 1993.

Packer, J.I. *God in Our Midst*. Word Books UK, 1987.

Paisley, Ian R K. *The Fifty-Nine Revival*. Free Presbyterian Church of Ulster: Belfast, 1959.

Sprange, Harry. *Children in Revival – Kingdom Kids*. Christian Focus Publications: Fearn, 1994.

Weir, John. *Heaven Came Down*. Ambassador: Belfast, 1860, 1987.

White, John. *When the Spirit Comes with Power*. Hodder & Stoughton: London, 1988, 1989, 1992.

Whittaker, Colin. *Great Revivals*. Marshall Pickering: London, 1984, 1990.

ALPHA

MAGAZINE

HELPING YOU SEE GOD AT WORK

IN EVANGELISM
News of creative evangelism and church growth from throughout the UK and around the world.

IN RENEWAL AND REFRESHING
Warm, thoughtful and indepth insights into revival and renewal from around the world. The most comprehensive reporting available.

IN PRAYER
Special features on intercession, personal prayer and local prayer strategies. Plus a 'ready to use' prayer guide for the UK and key mission fields abroad.

IN YOUR WORKPLACE
Regular Workwise features equip you to look at management, economic and ethical questions from a biblical perspective.

IN YOUR CHURCH
Steve Chalke writes for church leaders. Regular resource features help you discover the best practical advice on subjects as diverse as conference centres and concordances.

IN CULTURE
Reviews of key Christian books and music, and analysis of the arts and popular culture.

IN YOUR LIFE

Provocative, uplifting features help you on the path to Christian maturity.

 IN CURRENT ISSUES

Analysis of contemporary social issues, from euthanasia to the faith of politicians, from media influences to key Christian debates.

ALPHA brings you rich wisdom from across the Christian spectrum, from John Stott to John Wimber, from Clive Calver to Jim Packer, from Eleanor Kreider to Elaine Storkey.

To obtain ALPHA magazine hand the coupon below to your local Christian bookshop or church agent.

TO: BOOKSHOP / CHURCH AGENT

Please reserve me ....
copies of ALPHA until
further notice.

Name..

Address..

....

.... Postcode ....

BY POST

If you would prefer to have ALPHA sent by post, please write to: ALPHA magazine, FREEPOST, 37 Elm Road, New Malden, Surrey, KT3 3BR.

Please send me a .... year subscription to ALPHA starting with the .... issue. Enclosed is my payment (£23.70 - 1 year; £42.40 - 2 year*).

Name..

Address..

....

.... Postcode ....

1. I enclose a cheque for £............................ made payable to Elm House Christian Communications.

2. Please debit my credit card account with £............................

The access ☐ visa ☐ number is entered below.

Signature ....

Expiry date .... / ....

Or in case of difficulty write to Elm House Christian Communications for a sample copy and subscription details.

* This price applies to UK subscribers. Not usable in conjunction with any other offers. Prices stated are liable to change after July 1995. Overseas subscribers please note: payable by sterling draft or credit card only. Europe £30.70 (£56.40 - 2 year). Rest of the world £32.10 (£59.20 - 2 years). Elm House Christian Communications Ltd is registered under the Data Protection Act 1984 and holds names and addresses on computer for the purposes of mailing. Details on request.
☐ Tick here if you do not wish to receive mailings from other companies.